MICHAEL WILSON

The Church is Healing

SCM PRESS LTD
BLOOMSBURY STREET LONDON

To Mary
whose love and courage
made this book possible

FIRST PUBLISHED 1966
CHEAP EDITION 1967
© SCM PRESS LTD 1966
PRINTED IN GREAT BRITAIN BY
BILLING & SONS LIMITED
GUILDFORD AND LONDON

CONTENTS

5

CONTENTS

PREFACE

THIS book describes one way in which God is at work in the world today—healing. Men co-operate with him in many ways, religious and scientific, personal and social, within and without the Church.

The 'Church's Ministry of Healing' was a useful conception which helped to get rid of the mediaeval attitude of resignation to sickness and squalor. But it is now in danger of becoming a cult, with its own language, ritual and protected areas. Today, to write about the 'Church's Ministry of Healing' is to encounter the same difficulties as writing about the 'Church's Mission'. The word 'mission' has become associated with special societies, special collections, special parish activities, or journeys to a far country. Yet 'mission' is what the Church exists for. So the word 'healing' needs rescue from the specializers. For in the same sense that the Church *is* mission, the Church also *is* healing.

I am indebted to several friends who have read the first draft of this book and made many helpful suggestions: especially to the Rev. Canon R. E. C. Browne of Manchester, whose detailed criticisms and continued encouragement helped me very greatly. My helpers have added to the value of the book, but cannot be held responsible for its shortcomings.

I wish to thank Miss Rosemary Evans for typing the first draft, and my wife for typing the subsequent drafts and for much help with details. Old Testament quotations are from the Revised Standard Version: New Testament quotations are from the New English Bible.

M. W.

CHAPTER ONE

A DEFINITION OFFERED

JESUS'S works of healing were a normal part of his daily work. Where the Rule of God was being proclaimed, there the Lord healed. There was no special place, no special time, no special 'service'. There was for him nothing of the 'Healing Ministry at 8 p.m. on Wednesday evenings' approach. But where men and women live, work, and bring up their children, there the power of God is shown. There was in Jesus's work no separation of preaching and healing: his words healed, and his healing works loudly proclaimed the rule and purposes of God.[1]

Jesus's ways of healing were varied. There are several occasions recorded when Jesus healed all who came to him.[2] But it is striking how much care he took over individuals. We are told that he healed in many different ways. His word was with power, and the tone of authority in his dealings with sin and sickness was noted.[3] Sometimes he healed by the touch of his hand;[4] and if you want to convince a leper of the love of God, you can do it in no more certain way than by touching him: for the deep hunger of an untouchable's heart is to be touched; to belong again after being an outcast. Sometimes he healed by faith.[5] Per-

---

[1] Especially see: R. H. Fuller, *Interpreting the Miracles* (1963), pp. 40ff.; Dorothee Hoch, *Healing and Salvation* (1958); A. Richardson, *The Miracle Stories of the Gospels* (1941), p. 45; Jim Wilson, *Go Preach the Kingdom, Heal the Sick* (1962), ch. 2.

[2] Mark 1.32ff. (Matt. 8.16ff.; Luke 4.40ff.).

Mark 3.9ff. (Matt. 12.15; Luke 6.17ff.).

[3] Luke 4.36.   [4] Mark 1.41.   [5] Mark 5.34.

haps it was through the faith of those upon whom the sufferer was very dependent, as in the case of a child—her parents,[1] and in the case of a servant—his employer.[2] He healed a paralytic man by the forgiveness of his sins,[3] and a blind man by using clay and spittle, both of them then being used as native medicines.[4] Sometimes he healed in public,[5] sometimes in complete privacy.[6]

Just as Jesus worked with sick people in many different ways according to their need, so the Church today meets men's needs in many different ways.

In the Acts of the Apostles and the Epistles we see the development of Jesus's work by a community—the Church. The work of the Church is to proclaim the rule of God, as Jesus did. Each local church-community is to be his body, continuing his work locally. We are to be his hands, his feet, his lips, his eyes, in Wolverhampton, Bolgatanga, or Johannesburg. Not working independently, but together as a community; sometimes gathered together for the work of worship or prayer, sometimes scattered at work in the world as free agents, but always interdependent, always one. If we are faithful to this task, there will be associated with it the work of healing the sick.

The unit of the Church's healing work is the local congregation. As the Zulus say, 'When there is a thorn in the foot, the whole body must stoop to pluck it out'. But before we go any further it is necessary to describe what we mean by 'the Church' and what we mean by 'healing'.

WHAT IS THE CHURCH?

By 'Church' we mean not just a building, but the family of men and women who love the Lord Jesus Christ. The living members of the Church are ministers and laymen,

[1] Mark 7.29. [2] Matt. 8.10. [3] Mark 2.2ff.
[4] John 9.6. [5] Mark 1.32ff. [6] Mark 8.23.

husbands and wives, mothers, fathers, children; labourers and clerks; doctors and teachers; nurses and politicians; built together into one family in Christ. The Church's work is therefore the work of a very mixed community of people. And the Church's work is in the world. Within the church-building the Christian family worship God. They offer to him themselves, their life and work, and they are fed and fitted for duty in the world outside. They then go out into the world to carry out Christ's work in industry, education, commerce, hospital, politics and family life.

St Paul uses the image of *a loaf* to show something of the nature of the Church. He writes: 'Because there is one loaf, we, many as we are, are one body; for it is one loaf of which we all partake'.[1] He is thinking of the Communion loaf on the Lord's table: that loaf which is to be taken, blessed, broken and shared. At Holy Communion, we take this bread, and break it into pieces that each may receive his share. What we eat becomes a part of us; and we become a part of it. So the whole loaf now *is* the congregation. Each member is as intimately related to the other members of this Christian family as the bread within the loaf. We are one loaf: but we also become what we eat. We are one Body, his Body.

We can then take a map of our district, and work out on it where the loaf is on Monday morning. Let us put a small flag in the map where each piece of bread is at work in the world. Here's where George is at work in the bank, Mary at home with the children, John driving a bus, Helen nursing in the infirmary, and Harry a doctor out on his rounds. They are the loaf, feeding the world.

Dietrich Bonhoeffer writes:

> Everything the disciple does is part of the common life of the Church of which he is a member;[2]

[1] I Cor. 10.17.
[2] *The Cost of Discipleship* (first Eng. trs., 1948), p. 230.

and :

> . . . to stay in the world with God means simply to live in the rough and tumble of the world and at the same time remain in the Body of Christ, the visible Church, to take part in its worship and to live the life of discipleship.[1]

Yet 'church work' is often thought of in terms of cleaning the brass. This is, of course, entirely necessary; but if you are a mother who devotes her life to bringing up a family of five children in a Christian and godly way, finding little time for church organizations, it can be said of you, 'She does nothing for her church'. The phrase 'church worker' is often confined to one who has undergone special training and whose work lies more or less within the ecclesiastical set-up. Clearly such people are valuable. But if the term leads us to think that the Church is not involved in our daily work in the world, it would be better dropped. If a Christian nurse took up such training, it might be said of her that she had 'taken up church work' : whereas in fact she merely moves from one type of church work to another. If Helen is the only Christian nurse among half a dozen other girls on her ward, how this can bring alive the Bible image of 'leaven' or 'salt' at work in the world! Her worship on Sunday fits her for just this outpost where she works and witnesses for the rest of the week by her industry, patience and sensitivity to the needs of others.

Recently I heard a Christian surgeon talking to a gathering of clergy. He apologized for doing so little for his church —'one Bible class a month' as he put it. Yet here was a man who spent long hours daily in the hospital, setting men and women free from the burden of sickness. He had never seen this as anything to do with his church, and probably his church had never seen his work as anything to do with them.

[1] Ibid., p. 235.

St Paul uses another image to express truths about the Church. He speaks of us as *a body*—the Body of Christ, because the Spirit of Christ dwells in us and works through our hands.[1] So we are intimately dependent on one another and on Christ, who is the 'head' directing and energizing. Each member has his or her own special function, his or her own gift, in trust for the whole. Just as the eye does all the seeing for our body, and an ear all the hearing: so in Christ's Body one has a gift of 'wise speech', another 'faith', another 'healing', another 'prophecy'. We could add to St Paul's list gifts of public speaking, of sympathy, of a singing voice, of an artistic sense, and many others. Such gifts are not necessarily 'religious' in the churchy sense, but because these are gifts from God they are all to be used in his service. It is our responsibility to develop a gift industriously, to resist its prostitution, and to share it with others. There is no question of self-inflation or boasting about our gifts: they are held in trust for all.

Just as the whole of my body speaks through my lips, so the whole body of the Church (as it were) speaks through the lips of the Christian teacher in the day school. When the Christian community is gathered together on Sunday for prayer and the breaking of bread, each member is prepared by God for his work. What we receive on Sunday can become solid in the world on Monday morning through the lips of the teacher, the hands of the nurse, the love of the mother, the fairness of the employer, the industry of the employee. But what God is making us—persons in community—through the gift of his own life, is to be responsibly accepted, developed and shared with the world.

Among the members of the Church who go to work in the world, we know of some who are specially called and gifted with knowledge and skill for the curing of sick minds

[1] I Cor. 12.

and bodies: doctors and nurses, almoners, physiotherapists, and many professions associated with medicine. Their gifts of skill and knowledge are held in trust for the whole of society. But what they did with us, and we with them, on Sunday morning, has given new meaning to their healing work on Monday to Saturday. This is the Church's work in the world, in and through them—not just a personal career. In very truth, our hands are with the hands of Helen and Harry as they change dressings, operate and inject penicillin. Their daily work is now seen in its full context: and the power of the Church—the Body of Christ—is available in and through their daily handwork.

Although the relationship of those special professions to healing is obvious, health has other roots in many aspects of work and life. Who would deny that the mother of a family is a key person in the Church's work not just of healing but of teaching wholesome living? It is her love (and maybe her self affirmation, by putting home before job) which gives to her children their sense of being wanted and of security— those two essentials for sane growth of the mind. It is upon the mother of a family that the burden of sickness in a household falls. What endurance she needs to work hard in spite of sleepless nights! It is her own attitude of serenity and hope in the face of sickness which will often make for her child's recovery. If she knows in her hour of trial and weakness that she is not alone, but that she is a member of the Body, she receives him who heals and upholds. We can in the same way think of the work of teachers in the class-room, probation officers, child welfare workers, prison visitors and many professions dealing with broken lives. All have their place in the ministry of healing.

'And now,' says St Paul, 'I will show you the best way of all.' Then follows the great chapter, I Corinthians 13, which describes Christian love, the highest manifestation of God at work in the world.

I may have faith strong enough to move mountains; but if I have no love, I am nothing. . . . There is nothing love cannot face; there is no limit to its faith, its hope, and its endurance. Love will never come to an end.

We may think it strange that love is valued more highly than healing, yet Jesus taught this by his death and resurrection, the supreme victory of self-giving love. Only a community based on the love described by St Paul could be trusted with the gifts of the Spirit. Only a community which was trying to express this self-giving love for others could face the testing situations which in this life are not changed, but must be accepted. Many claim faith enough to be healed; but few aspire to the love which can face anything.

The love of the church-community means that we ought to take one another on for better or for worse, for always. And a member who continues long in sickness or disability will test the Church to the uttermost. To undertake intercession for a sick man may mean we have to see the family through a difficult time. We may have to see a man's widow and children through their adjustment to life after his death —not just spiritually, but materially too. Every member of the congregation will be the better or the worse for accepting or refusing such responsibility. Intercession will not merely demand this of us, but will do this to us.

So we see the Church as a family of those who love the Lord Jesus Christ. We are his agents in this twentieth-century world, through whom he can care for the vagrant; stand by the alcoholic; mend broken marriages, broken minds or broken bodies. Each local church must take up the work to which it is called in its locality, and adapt the pattern of its life accordingly. For example, how wrong it could be to spend all our efforts on collecting money for leprosy patients overseas, and to neglect a local mental hospital which wants visitors and hostesses for long-stay patients! (A church might, of course, do both: in fact it is often those whose charity has already begun at home who have enough and to spare for those in need afar off.) How wrong it could be to concentrate on intercession for the sick when the local situation requiring prayer is youth work or race relations; and while the strong and the beautiful often need prayer just as much as the weak. The Church as a community is always alive, and like living organisms shows a constant ability to learn, to grow, and adapt to meet new demands. Rigidity is one of the signs of death.

WHAT IS HEALING?

The most obvious meaning of the word 'heal' as we might use it in common parlance is to 'cure'. The word 'heal' is not one which would come easily to the lips of a General Practitioner in his surgery: nor would it normally be used to describe the work of a hospital. A doctor 'cures': a cut on my finger 'heals'.

If a woman comes to her General Practitioner with boils, he cures her. What is involved is a restoration to function. A General Practitioner who is competent at restoring his patients to full activity is doing his job well, as a technician. Such work is co-operating with God naturally—in and through nature—and is acceptable to him. As a man, of course, the doctor is not a robot, but human, and he cannot escape the implications of personal relationship to his patients. This introduces personal and often mysterious factors into the healing situation.

The word 'cure' or 'treat' is also used in the New Testament of many of Jesus's works. (A Greek word which is often used is the root from which our 'therapy' comes.) 'Jesus went round . . . curing whatever illness or infirmity there was among the people.'[1] This way of looking at sick-

[1] Matt. 4.23.

ness and healing is very common and underlies much of our theology about healing. But its individualism is quite foreign to the Jewish mind, and increasingly old-fashioned in medical circles today.

Today we know that it is better to think of man as a social creature, as a person in relationship to others. A definition of 'cure' as 'restoration to function' lacks social content. Disease has its roots in a patient's life and relationships; if not causally, certainly as an event which affects the lives of others. Both to the biblical writers and to the twentieth century doctor, sickness is a situation which involves the whole family. The cure of mental sickness, for example, requires social rehabilitation in family, church, club and work situations. We can therefore define the word 'cure' as 'restoration to function *in society*'. The word 'heal', as used by Christians, contains in addition a reference to the purpose of life; to God's purpose for this patient's life. The surgeon may restore an injured hand to function : 'healing' looks at the hand as part of a person-in-relationship, and is concerned for the purpose, loving or hating, to which the restored hand is put.

It is evident therefore that any view of sickness (or health) which sees it in terms of static pathology, rather than as a dynamic process, is now out of date. A stay in hospital is an unusual event in a long sequence from life before to life afterwards. We must not approach a sick person as if he was a still photograph, but rather as a moving picture. Life is continuous, and sickness is not a pause in it, but a creative or destructive period of life. We meet the sick man in the middle of this living process : we are to try to understand what went before, and to help him to respond creatively.

Dr R. A. Lambourne has suggested the following definition for healing : 'Healing is a satisfactory response to a crisis, made by a group of people, both individually and corporately.'[1] This definition has the advantage of approaching sickness as only one manifestation of evil in the world. It emphasizes how those who surround the patient—family, friends, doctor, nurse, minister, probation officer and others —are all involved in the situation with him. For all of them sickness is a learning situation, a crisis event, and an opportunity for progress or regress. All are the better or the worse for having to live the situation through whether it be sickness, bereavement, earthquake, or imprisonment. None of them emerges from the situation as the same person, and their response to future crises will be influenced by what they have learnt in this one. Not as an alternative to Dr Lambourne's definition, but as a further description of what we mean by 'satisfactory response', we can say that healing means *restoration to purposeful living in society*.

Any conception of 'curing' is, therefore, embraced within the word 'heal', and given purpose. On the other hand, because physical health subserves the purpose of life— loving God, loving neighbour, loving self—it is legitimate to use the word 'healed' of someone who has been enabled to take up a life of self-giving, without having been cured physically. Christians might here use the word 'saved' in its place. It is ultimately style of life which is important, not perfection of form; loving rather than being intact. That there is a way in which we are to 'love ourselves' is often overlooked: but in fact we can only love our neighbours in so far as we love ourselves. And the loving acceptance of mutilation or limitation may be a necessary step to our freedom to care for others.

Dr Lambourne has also pointed out that the word *sōzein* in the New Testament is used to mean both 'saved' in a theological context, and 'made whole' in a medical context.[2] The words 'whole' and 'wholeness' are used to de-

[1] *Frontier*, vol. 6, no. 1 (Spring 1963).
[2] R. A. Lambourne, *Community, Church and Healing* (1963), Ch. 8.

scribe a state of being towards which we grow, when all shall be one in Christ.[1] It is that fullness of life which we shall realize together when God's purpose is accomplished, and his Kingdom proclaimed in all its fullness. Some psychiatrists speak of integration of the person as the process of 'wholing'. In Christian thought also, 'wholeness' suggests something (though in a wider sense) towards which we all move both severally and together. It is a dynamic, not a static, concept.

The word *sōzein*, both theological and medical, therefore points to the truth that through Christ we may enter into wholeness of life—however imperfectly—now. In a world in which ageing and death are common human experience, 'wholeness' is more related to a quality of Christian living than to bodily perfection. For in this life we have this treasure in earthen vessels: wholeness belongs to the end of history, when all created matter has become obedient to God, and we really do love God with all our heart, with all our soul, with all our mind, and with all our strength, and our neighbours as ourselves.

[1] Eph. 4.13ff.

CHAPTER TWO

THE CHURCH GATHERS FOR
HEALING

MAN is, of his very nature, a social creature. Man is family man. It is human to meet one another and live together: alone we are incomplete. We grow to maturity as an independent person by the give and take of encounter with other persons; this takes place most naturally in the family first, then in a widening circle of friends and casual contacts. Life, therefore, fully human life, is life-together. This is a natural association which God has made and through which he expresses his nature.

But human society is divided by jealousy, ambition, domination, and hatred. Such attitudes are the root causes of many social problems such as *apartheid* between races, separation by an iron curtain, the division of one church from another, the divorce of husband and wife. These five spheres of life-together, racial, political, economic, religious and sexual, are torn by divisions—but in Christ there can be reconciliation.

The twelve disciples would not have described their association with Jesus as a peaceful experience. There were James and John, nicknamed 'Sons of Thunder', fiery in temperament. There was Peter who three times denied that he even knew Jesus; capable of the highest vision and the most squalid cowardice. Judas stole money from the common purse and finally betrayed him. There were Simon the Zealot, whose party vows required him to knife anyone who

co-operated with the Romans; and Matthew who had col-
lected taxes for the Romans. It must have been a tense
experience holding these two together in the same company. Even at the last supper they were quarrelling about
which of them was to be greatest. But Jesus held them
together. This experience of life, being held together by
Jesus, in a company which accepts difference and transcends division, is what we mean by Christian fellowship.
Both in the world and in the Church we find groups of
people whose fellowship together depends upon similarity
of temperament and uniformity of practice. They choose
one another. This is a natural association, beyond which
many people cannot or will not go. But in Christian community we are given to one another, we do not choose one
another. Our fellowship is not sinless: nor does it depend
upon sinlessness for its continuance, but upon forgiveness.
Christian fellowship must hold together—sometimes in a
tension which is to be borne—men of different viewpoint.
True maturity accepts that our knowledge is partial and
that man and woman together, or Anglican and Presbyterian together, or Englishman and Negro together, supple-
ment their own particular (but partial) insights. Unity, not
uniformity, gives richness to Christian fellowship.

A working party studying Christian work among nurses
today writes in their report:

> Almost all Christian organizations for nurses rate fellow-
> ship highly among those things which they offer. It is a dis-
> turbing anomaly that nurses' groups which speak most loudly
> of 'fellowship' are among the most exclusive. What do we
> mean by 'fellowship'?
>
> If we are content with the happy glow which warms us
> when birds of a feather flock together, then we shall miss the
> deeper, more disturbing experience which the disciples knew
> from being together with Jesus. Fellowship does not depend
> on the exclusion of those who disagree with us.[1]

[1] *Christianity and Nursing Today* (1964), p. 26.

When St Paul wrote that 'there is no such thing as Jew and Greek, slave and freeman, male and female; for you are all one person in Christ Jesus',[1] he was not theorizing. He was bearing witness to the power of Christian fellowship. It was the same power which could bring together Chinese and Japanese Christians to meet together while their countries were at war. It is the same power in South Africa today which seeks to break down barriers of apartheid, and which has inspired the work of Trevor Huddleston, Ambrose Reeves and Hannah Stanton. In the United States of America the work of reconciliation between Negroes and whites by Martin Luther King has its power from the same source.

PARTICIPATION AND ACCEPTANCE

In any group of people, individual contributions of speech and silence vary. Some members of the group speak freely and often: other members are more reflective. It is characteristic of a mature man or woman to be able to *participate*, to give themselves, to share in a fellowship, whether through speech or silence. And it is important to respect silence; and not to force a reflective person to speak unwillingly, or to feel guilty about their true role of silence.

Some people may have difficulty in making personal relationships. Perhaps way back in childhood, or during adolescence, the first shy attempts at meeting another were refused, laughed at or even deliberately crushed. The unfolding bud of relationship then closed its sepals tightly again. In the group, only when others accept a person, and he (or she) finds himself in a secure environment, is he able to go back to the point where he closed his sepals, and begin to open them again. Then indeed he begins to unfold, to grow, to share: and before our eyes a new person is born.

[1] Gal. 3.28.

For it *is* characteristic of a mature man or woman to be able to participate, to give themselves, to share in a fellowship. And every one of us, however bent or broken, has got a unique contribution to make to the church-community : a contribution which no one else under heaven can make.'

This growth in the capacity for relationship is one of the most fascinating aspects of the healing work which can take place in small group meetings. Nevertheless group work is difficult, and requires skilled leadership. For acceptance is not an easy thing. To *accept* someone is to take them as we find them, for better or for worse : to be ready to bear, without condemnation, all that another's weakness or hostility may do to me. To accept a man is to care for him as Bill, just because he is Bill.

In my own experience there are some people who always seem to bring out a particular fault in me; they always think of me as that person with that fault. They cannot heal me : on the contrary they bind my faults to me. And there are other people in whose presence I am free to be myself, because they love me for who I am. These are the ones who accept me. It is they who can help me to overcome my faults.

Acceptance is the basis of all lasting relationship, and is therefore embedded in the Marriage Service of the Book of Common Prayer :

> I, John, take thee, Jane, to my wedded wife, to have and to hold from this day forward, for better, for worse : for richer, for poorer; in sickness and in health; to love and to cherish, till death us do part. . . .

This aims to provide a loving environment in which children may be brought up without fear of rejection because of their 'badness'. Family life shows u‚ in miniature what the Church is called to become : not a perfect community, but a *family* whose members love us. It is a test of true fellowship when our friends know the worst about us and remain our friends.

The World Council of Churches gathered at Evanston in 1954 sent a message to all congregations throughout the world, which included this question: *Is your congregation a true family of God where every man may come and find a welcome and know that God loves him without limit?* In most Christian congregations the answer is 'No'. In few parishes or churches are there groups of people able to work together as a 'true family of God', and it is therefore significant that some of the healing work through fellowship in the Church today is being pioneered by extra-parochial 'families of God'. The 'love of God' can easily remain an empty pious phrase unless it is visible and tangible in the caring of a group of people. If we disciples care enough, maybe those who say 'there's a God of love for you but not for me' will catch a glimpse in us and through us and beyond us of a God who cares for *them*. Yet men do not always respond to love. Jesus warned that his disciples might be ignored or stoned. It is a true test of the quality of love to have to face its own rejection.

Describing the work of a Community Therapy Unit for the rehabilitation of mental patients, Dr Denis Martin writes:

> Let us really believe in the power of love to resolve conflict within and without. But let us never sentimentalize it. Initially real goodness, which is love, is often met with hostility and fear because it reveals in us things that are too painful to accept. This makes it feel as if love is a hard and cruel thing, but we turn love into sentimentality if we try to empty it of this harsher aspect. The judgement of God is what it feels like when we resist or reject it. If love receives hostility without resentment or self-pity, and goes on loving and receiving, in the end it will prove redemptive and release healing, for love never fails. But we must be clear that often and often it seems to fail. To many the cross was the greatest failure of history. In our community units, we have this

experience of failure; patients sometimes leave us abruptly in a mood of resentment, hostility and blaming us for not helping them. . . . Such patients would have stayed with us if we let them have a nice rest, providing everything for them and helping them to cover up their conflicts and their sin. This was the old traditional way of treatment. The same experience will be suffered by the church if accepting sacrificial love is really released and experienced. It will split the conventional, respectable church down the middle, people will be offended and will leave. Real love is a costly and dangerous thing, but Jesus made it quite clear that we must lose our lives if we would save them. We cannot pray behind locked doors, we must go out and share the often costly and painful experience of healing with them, confident that God goes with us and his healing power is sufficient to cover our deficiencies. We cannot save ourselves or others from the costs of healing; the way of Jesus was the way of sharing the experience with men and women, not of protecting them or himself from it.[1]

In a later book[2] Dr Martin has described how such a revolutionary approach to personal relationships between patients and staff, and among the staff themselves, began the slow and painful disappearance of the old hierarchical way of running a mental hospital. Personal relationships were enabled to subserve the whole pattern of therapy and rehabilitation. Interestingly enough some of the violent symptoms so long associated with mental illness were found to be due to the old suppressive type of régime, and disappeared in the new permissive atmosphere of understanding.

A description of the way in which members of a local Baptist church have co-operated at this hospital in the work of helping long-stay patients to recovery, by caring for them in co-operation with the hospital staff, has been published.[3]

Caring for the sick has been the work of religious communities down the centuries, and today there are many

[1] Denis Martin, *The Church as a Healing Community* (1958), p. 11.
[2] Denis Martin, *Adventures in Psychiatry* (1962).
[3] L. M. Barrett in *Occupational Therapy*, November 1960.

religious orders, both Roman Catholic and Anglican, which are deeply involved in healing work. In the Church of England, for example, the Community of St Mary the Virgin, Wantage, does a variety of work for the sick, the elderly and the feeble-minded. The Community of the Nursing Sisters of St John the Divine, Hastings, find expression of their dedication to God in the care of the sick and suffering. A number of Anglican religious orders undertake medical work overseas; for example, the Order of the Holy Paraclete, Whitby, runs a Maternity Teaching Hospital in Ghana, and the Community of the Sacred Passion does extensive teaching and nursing work in East Africa. Others work with maladjusted or homeless children : for example, the Society of St Francis, Cerne Abbas, offers help to men and lads in trouble.

The principle of care in groups or family units has been worked out for particular needs by organizations like Alcoholics Anonymous,[1] and the Richmond Fellowship.[2] The Pilsdon Community in Dorset live together, work together, and worship together as a family.[3] Their life is modelled on the example of Nicholas Ferrar at Little Gidding in the seventeenth century. They help men and women who have reached breaking point to accept themselves and others as they are, and so to discover something of what life-together means. The Community adopted as a motto the words from the lamp in the canoe which brings patients to Dr Schweitzer's Hospital at Lambarene in West Africa : *Here at all times of the day and night are light and help and human kindness.*

Such an accepting family life, in home or church or community, has power to heal. But love is disinterested. We do not love because it heals. We love people because this is

---

[1] *Alcoholics Anonymous* (World's Work, 1964).   [2] See p. 112.
[3] P. Smith, *Towards Life Together* (Pilsdon Manor, Bridport, Dorset).

what it means to be fully human, made in the image of God. Love must make its appeal to free spirits—and love does not call out love inevitably.

OUR RELATIONSHIP WITH GOD

Prayer is the work of the church-community. It is a work which opens both individuals and groups to the personal action of the Holy Spirit. It is therefore guiding, enlightening, strengthening, convicting, healing, disturbing and changing. It is an inner togetherness with God: a personal meeting. It belongs first to the realm of being fully alive. At first sight this is strange, when our prayers consist so often in doing something: in speaking, in listening, in adoring, in asking. Yet at the heart of them all is a personal meeting, a relationship towards which prayer activities lead, and from which prayer activities spring. The very first stumbling, groping prayer is a sign that God is already at work in us, creating and fostering the very desire to pray. Prayer, whether silent or spoken, arises from this inner togetherness: 'saying our prayers' is an expression of that relationship. And in turn 'saying our prayers' feeds that inner relationship deep within our very being, and helps it to grow and flourish.

Eight years ago, when my wife had been in and out of hospital a number of times, she received a letter from which she knew that she would have to go back. She told no one at the time. But our youngest son, who was then four, was like a bear with a sore head all morning: he would not leave her. Towards lunchtime in the kitchen, hanging on to her apron, he suddenly burst into tears and said: 'Don't go back into hospital, Mummy, don't go back into hospital.' This is an example of communion—a wordless kinship—between two beings: an inner togetherness which does not need to be informed, but *knows*. So the heart of prayer is

27

communion, something deeper than communication, deeper than 'saying our prayers'. For at all times within and through our speaking and our listening, GOD IS.

This point is made first as a bulwark against too much concern over prayer techniques. Important as these may be, prayer which is not first seeking to know and love God himself easily gets sidetracked into discussions about 'suggestion' or 'telepathy'; and worse still, when considering intercessions, into clinical details about somebody's glandular deficiencies. The way we pray depends upon what we think about God. For Christians, God is as we see him in Jesus: 'Anyone who has seen me has seen the Father.'[1] And in Jesus we see four things which will influence our whole approach to sick people: the goodness of God, his love, his continuing activity, and his constant presence.

1. *God is good*. God is as we see him in Jesus: a comforter of widows, a healer of the sick, a merciful judge, a friend of outcasts, a scourge of hypocrites. But day after day we shall face situations in life which apparently deny God's goodness. We meet a young mother with cancer, a spastic child, or a mongol baby. Can we retain undimmed our trust in God, rooted in a knowledge of his utter goodness? Our knowledge of God's goodness rests upon what we see in Jesus, and our own acceptance of this by faith is strengthened through prayer, meditation, Bible reading and the sacraments. When we know God is utterly good and trustworthy, then we are able to look at life with discerning eyes. Only then can we see those things which are of God, and those things which are spoiling his creation. And it is upon this God-given discernment of goodness, and of God's good purpose, that our efforts to overcome suffering depend.

As Paul Tillich wrote:

Christianity knows that such a victory over destructive

[1] John 14.9.

28

suffering is only partly possible in time and space. But whether this fragmentary victory is fought for or not makes all the difference between Western and Eastern cultures, as a comparison shows. It changes the valuation of the individual, of personality, of community and of history. It has in fact, determined the historical destiny of mankind.[1]

The conviction of God's goodness grows through prayer, and it shapes not only our prayers but our whole attitude to sin and sickness. It made possible the first hospitals, with an altar at the end of the ward. It opened the way for our modern endeavour against sickness throughout the world, in sure confidence that this is an evil to be overcome. So an unshakable faith in the goodness of God will influence the way we pray; we shall not have to beg him to heal a sick child as if he had never thought of such an idea. For God is good like Jesus.

2. *God is present.* Jesus said : 'And be assured, I am with you always, to the end of time.'[2] Here is a promise on which we may rely. We shall not need to pray to God as if he was far off. He is closer than breathing, and 'nearer than hands and feet'. We know he hears and will answer.

We know too, that he is among us when we meet as his Body, the Church. And when praying for others we remember that Christ is also present with them. Perhaps our prayers can help them to become aware of him, to let him have his way with them, to yield to the loving power of his Holy Spirit within them.

During our lives, there are moments of awareness of the presence of God: at Holy Communion, in a prayer group, in the silence of deep country, in the face of a friend. But he is just as present when we are not aware of him. He is just as present in the racket of a hospital out-patient department or in the searing din of a steelworks; for he is at the heart of life, of all that is. It is also in times of doubt and dark-

[1] Paul Tillich, *Systematic Theology* (1953-57), vol. ii, p. 81.
[2] Matt. 28.20.

ness that we must trust that he is present, independently of our feelings. It is obvious that although a sharp attack of 'flu' depresses our feelings in prayer, yet it makes no difference to the presence of God.

3. *God cares*. We see Jesus's deep care for people in his healing works, in his merciful forgiveness of sinners, in his blessing of children and in his willingness to die for his friends. In the face of great suffering, or when frustrated by an insoluble problem, when words fail us we may only be able to point to the Cross and say: 'God cares here and now, that much.'

We, too, must care. We have seen how care for people is one of the roots from which a ministry of healing can grow. It is even more important than faith: 'I may have faith strong enough to move mountains; but if I have no love, I am nothing.'[1] Prayer deepens our care for people: and our care for people deepens our prayers for them and gives us perseverance.

4. *God is at work*. 'My Father has never yet ceased his work, and I am working too.'[2] Jesus showed us the works of God. 'He went about doing good'[3]: healing, forgiving, binding up, laying down his life, making crooked things straight in human minds and bodies as well as relationships. Now, as then, God continues to work out his purpose in and through faithful followers, in and through the church-community, in and through history, in and through all that he has made and is making. Prayer is one way of co-operating with him in the everyday world, today.

God is at work. But we also have our part to play, as St James makes clear:

> Suppose a brother or a sister is in rags with not enough food for the day, and one of you says 'Good luck to you, keep yourselves warm, and have plenty to eat', but does nothing to supply their bodily needs, what is the good of that?[4]

[1] I Cor. 13.2   [2] John 5.17.   [3] Acts 10.38.   [4] James 2.15.

30

We hold in balance this commonsense teaching about our own co-operation, with a real faith in God's power so simply expressed by Fénelon : *Let God act!*

How do these four glimpses into the heart of God shape our prayers, and also our words to those who need comfort? A teacher of prayer has asked : 'Why do we pray "Thy will be done" so often at funerals, but so rarely at weddings?' Yet if we believe that God is as we have seen him in Jesus, then surely when his will is done, on earth as in heaven, that is the most wonderful thing that could possibly happen. We pray this prayer, not in fear or resignation because of the tragedy of the situation, but in hope and faith because God is as he is—like Jesus. The resignation or hope in our prayers betrays what we believe about God.

INTERCESSION

In any discussion of prayer as related to healing, we inevitably plunge into a consideration of intercession. But this short introduction above, putting God first as we see him in Jesus, will remind us of what we may otherwise overlook, that intercession is set in its right place and proportion in the whole work and worship of the Church.

We belong to one another; there is no such thing as being a separate person. The opening words of the Lord's Prayer, 'Our Father', underline our interdependence in prayer as in life. There is in effect no such thing as selfish prayer : selfish prayer is stillborn. Jesus taught : 'When you pray, go into a room by yourself, shut the door, and pray to your Father who is there in the secret place.'[1] Lex Miller used to say : 'But before you shut the door, go into the street, and see if there's a brother there you can take in with you.' This shows a Christlike insight into the nature of man. For

[1] Matt. 6.6.

I cannot in fact shut my brother out: there is no life for me without my brother: without him there is no completeness for me, and I even need him to know God more fully. 'If he does not love the brother whom he has seen, it cannot be that he loves God whom he has not seen.'[1]

In my own private prayer life, then, I may or may not find privacy—Jesus must have had little or none in his own home—but I can find a secret place for quiet. There I wrestle not just for myself, but for my brother, too. Because we are interdependent no action is private. We share with one another whatever God gives to us during our communion with him. Therefore the fruits of private prayer are common property in daily living. It will make all the difference to the man in the corner bed of a hospital ward whether his nurse has prayed before she went on duty or not, although he may not have been the subject of her prayers. For the test of her prayer is in the quality of her living—and nursing—when she rises from her knees.

Perhaps the ineffectiveness of so much intercessory prayer for others lies not in the poverty of our services of intercession, but in what we are *not* doing between one gathering and the next. It is not enough to pray 'Thy will be done in and through my brother in need' once a week or even daily, unless we know the cost of that prayer by the sweat of our own brow in our own daily obedience. In prayer, therefore, because of the family nature of man, we are linked together. To pray is to pray with: to pray is to pray for.

But if we also think of prayer as primarily a personal meeting with God, we can see intercession arising naturally from this. To meet one who is Holiness-in-action draws me into the wholing activity of God as a co-operator. It is not enough—here on earth in this age—to enjoy God: to be with God is to work with God. Therefore to pray is to be

[1] I John 4.20.

involved in a healing ministry because of what God is. We do not take up healing as if it was a special interest of a few of us. We are *all of us* involved in the healing of the world because of what God is like as seen in Jesus; because prayer is to enter into the activity of God and to co-operate with him in the purpose of his Kingdom; because this is not just my private interest but concerns my brother whom I cannot forget in the presence of God. That spastic child, that broken home, that starved refugee, that prisoner in Johannesburg, are part of me in my communion with God —because of what God is as seen in Jesus on the Cross : and because of what I am made by God to be, his child, not in isolation—but in solidarity with his other children.

Intercession has been defined as *meeting God about my brother's business*. We do not need to inform him in great detail of John's or Mary's business, for 'Your Father knows what your needs are before you ask him'.[1] But we must not leave it vague and pious, for Jesus taught us to come to God as a loving Father who knows how to give good gifts to his children. St James might have said : 'It's no use merely praying for refugees "Be ye warmed" if you can do something about blankets.' So the intercessors in the local church need to *say* their intercessions on their knees, and then go and *do* their intercessions by visiting and caring for those about whom they meet God. Common to both doing and saying our prayers is that inner togetherness with God which reaches out with compassion into daily life. Prayer and care are different ways of participating in the same creative activity of co-operation with a God of compassion. On the other hand, it is part of the tragedy of life that it is not always possible to take direct action on behalf of others. As a nurse's prayer for her patient may be in an extra gentleness of her hands, so the prayer of a congregation for

[1] Matt. 6.8.

someone in need of healing may be in a readiness to accept one who repels, or in humble willingness to see a man (and his family) through a time of breakdown. A man who prays, a cell or a church which prays, become the focal point of God's activity, where he is. Prayer works! Or rather, God works in and through us.

Thanksgiving[1] is a neglected aspect of prayer in the ministry of healing, and far fewer people remember to give thanks than are eager to ask for our prayers. Yet not only personal thanks are important, but thanksgiving is one of the keys to acknowledging the presence and activity of God in modern medicine. Much present-day treatment is so swift and sure that intercession is superfluous. For doctors and nurses, life-giving procedures are commonplace and routine: after all the thing works whether you pray or not.

This is the point at which either these works of cure slip out of God's sovereignty, or we recognize that thanksgiving is now the form of prayer which is needed. Our generation will hardly be giving thanks for the conquest of cholera, in Britain, although our fathers did. Our sons will not remember the conquest of diphtheria and tuberculosis, although we do. Each generation has such great thanksgivings to offer. They are important prayers which teach us to note the finger of God in the things of daily life, and to keep material blessings under the rule of God.

THE LAYING ON OF HANDS

The 'laying on of hands' is used in two ways for ministry to the sick: as an act of the Church by placing hands upon the head with prayer, and as an act of cure by someone with a physical gift of healing, when the hands are laid upon the sick part of the body. These two ways may or may not be combined.

[1] See also p. 58.

As an act of the Church, the laying on of hands has been used since ancient times to convey power and authority. It is an outward and visible sign whereby an inward blessing or power is conveyed. In the Old Testament it was used by Moses to convey authority to his successor, Joshua.[1] Jacob used it to bless Joseph's sons.[2] In the gospels Jesus is described as using it to bless little children,[3] to heal the sick,[4] and to cleanse a leper.[5] The practice is referred to in the commission to the disciples: 'They shall lay hands upon the sick.'[6] In the Acts of the Apostles the laying on of hands is given for the gift of the Holy Spirit after baptism,[7] for healing,[8] as a missionary commission,[9] and for ordination of the seven deacons.[10] In the Epistles it is referred to as the means of ordination.[11] It has, therefore, many uses, but the intention is always clear. There is, in the Bible, no suggestion of its use in a vague way for uplift. Today it is used by the Church with a similar variety of intentions for blessing, commissioning, healing, 'confirmation', and ordination.

The minister's hands are the hands of the whole Church. When a minister at the Lord's Table takes bread and breaks it, at that moment all the hands of the whole congregation are with his hands in the breaking. It is the whole Church who through his hands takes and breaks the bread. In and through his Body, the Church, Christ himself, once again, takes and breaks. In the same way when the minister lays his hands upon the head of a sick person, it is as if the hands of all the congregation are with his hands, focusing their love and prayers for the one in need. It is a corporate act of the Church as the Christ-indwelt community. The right person to give the laying on of hands is, therefore, that local community's own minister. He can prepare the one in need

[1] Num. 27.18. [2] Gen. 48.14. [3] Matt. 19.15.
[4] Luke 4.40. [5] Mark 1.41. [6] Mark 16.18.
[7] Acts 8.17. [8] Acts 9.17. [9] Acts 13.3.
[10] Acts 6.6. [11] I Tim. 4.14, 5.22.

and continue to follow up this ministry with the help of the congregation through friendship and visiting.

Implicit in such a community's act is commitment: our commitment to the sick man. As we lay hands upon him we express our love, which is not just a feeling, but a way of saying, 'You belong to us, we belong to you, for better or for worse: whatever happens we will care for you.' Whether the patient lives or dies we shall learn what that love means: for the congregation which has laid its hands upon someone and is committed to him in love must care for him and his family. Such care and concern can set a patient free of all anxiety. So he becomes more fully conscious of God's love within the community and can respond to it. He can trust God as the very source of his own life and health, deep within himself.

The laying on of hands is, therefore, an act through which the Holy Spirit within a community expresses his love. If introduced as a healing act without a caring Body behind it, there is a risk of its being a dead ceremony. It may then be merely the expression of a magical idea of a God who intervenes from outside. In my own ministry I do not lay hands on the sick at public healing services, because I have always felt it right to make this act a responsible one for the local community. It seems to me right to meet the one in need, even if only for a short time, to help them to respond to our Lord without anxiety, and also to discover whether the laying on of hands would in fact be the right way to meet their need. I try to avoid anything which will dilute the importance and responsibility of the act both for the local church who lay on hands, and for the patient. There is, however, a wide variety of custom and practice in the Church, and the Holy Spirit is not frustrated by our inadequate methods as long as we seek to co-operate with his love.

The laying on of hands is an act which may vary from a

simple placing of hands upon the patient's head when praying with him in hospital, to a formal occasion at Holy Communion in the face of the congregation. I like to have at
least one or two friends or members of the prayer group
present to remind both patient and myself of the presence
of the Church; but this is not always possible. Any way
forward towards recovering this act of healing in the Church
seems to me to lie in deepening the care of the local church-
community. God acts through a community which accepts
the cost of making such love real for *this* person in *this*
place, *now*.[1]

THE SACRAMENTS

So much has been written on the sacraments as a means
of healing that no attempt will be made here to repeat
orthodox teaching.[2] A few notes may recommend a fresh
emphasis on neglected aspects.

The World Health Organization has pointed out that the
commonest cause of disease in the world is still poverty.
There is no medicine in the world today with as great power
to remake the bodies of men, women and children as loaves
of bread (thinking here of bread as a symbol for food: it is,
if we are being literal, not only calories but especially pro-
tein and vitamins that are needed). But gifts of food in the
form of charity often degrade both giver and receiver. What
will men not do for bread? How often gifts are given with
strings attached: if you will sing this hymn, you may drink
this plate of soup or attend this school. So, in the world

[1] For an account of the laying on of hands as an act of cure by
someone with a physical gift of healing, see Leslie Weatherhead,
Psychology, Religion and Healing (1951), pp. 144ff.
[2] In *Liturgy and Worship*, ed. W. K. Lowther Clarke (1932), there
is a chapter by Harris entitled 'Visitation of the Sick', which is a
classic. See also A. H. Purcell Fox, *The Church's Ministry of Healing* (1959).

today, the backward countries have come to hate those who have given them most. Bread given and received may divide rather than reconcile.

Jesus saw this in the first temptation in the wilderness; and he who had all to give refused to win men's 'Yes' by universal provision. Yet at the heart of his new society Jesus set a fellowship meal of broken bread. For he chose the way, not of *giving* bread but of *sharing* it. Christ's way is participation in and with. St Martin was truly Christlike when, instead of pulling off his cloak and throwing it to the naked beggar, he took his sword and cut it in half to share it with him. There is no hurt in this way of giving and receiving, only healing. To share our very own loaf with a man in need feeds him body and soul. It is an act of feeding by mouth; it is an act of feeding by fellowship. It unites and does not divide. It uplifts and does not degrade. It heals and does not wound. *And the Church is the great bread-sharing community of the world*. Christ meets us in our need for both bread and a brother.

Perhaps the most outstanding work of healing done by the Church since the war has been the feeding and rehabilitation of refugees through Christian Aid. Feeding hungry people is part of the Church's ministry of healing, and Jesus's chosen method is by sharing. Do we in the West who eat 3,000 calories a day, pray for hungry peoples who get 1,500 calories a day without sharing what we have? Do we share bread equally at the Lord's table, but not outside the Church? There is no sharing without breaking. 'At the very centre of our religion there are scraps of broken bread.'[1]

Communion for the sick at home or in hospital can be linked to the Holy Communion of the Church in a way that brings out our corporate concern for the sick. In a parish in Lancashire they use a printed Communion card for sick

[1] R. E. C. Browne, *Meditations on the Temptations and Passion of Our Lord* (1955), chap. 5.

people which has on it a picture of the altar in the parish church. This is to bring to mind the Lord's house where the Lord's people meet on the Lord's day to break bread together. At that service enough bread and wine are laid aside for the sick. Then just as the priest on Sunday comes down from the altar to the altar rail to give bread to the people, so later he comes down from this same altar bringing the same bread along the streets of his parish to those laid up at home. The service at home is a continued part of the family service in the church : the church-community is not broken. In some such way as this, we can try to save Sick Communion from becoming that contradiction in terms, a private Communion.

The Anointing of the Sick.[1] A sacrament reveals at a particular time and place the relationship between spirit and matter. One minor sacrament, anointing with oil, is concerned with the healing of the sick, based upon its use by the disciples in the Early Church for this purpose.[2] In the use of olive oil in this way there were two interwoven lines of thought. There was the idea of consecration, from the use of oil in the consecration of Jewish priests and kings and later from Christian initiation. But also olive oil was familiar in the home for cooking, lighting, and as a homely remedy for oiling of the skin and rubbing into aches and pains.

In the Early Church the sick were not just signed with the sign of the Cross when anointed, as is customary today, but there are records of the whole body being anointed with oil (blessed by the bishop) and of repeated daily anointing with steadfast prayer.[3] Both the sick man's medicines and

---

[1] Parts of this section appeared in *Theology*, vol. lxiii (May-June 1960), and are reprinted by kind permission of the Editor and the SPCK.

[2] Mark 6.13; James 5.14.

[3] F. W. Puller, *Anointing of the Sick in Scripture and Tradition* (1910), pp. 155ff.

his food (especially his bread, wine and grapes) and water
were blessed by the bishop or presbyter.[1] In addition, the
anointing was carried out in the presence of the local
church.

So the Early Church saw things much more whole than
we do. The patient's relationships and everything that supported his life (food and drink), or was for his healing
(medicines), were taken and acknowledged as gifts of the
Holy Spirit, to be consecrated for his work of re-creation.
Everything, even a cup of cold water, could be a means of
spiritual blessing. Natural and supernatural, spiritual and
physical, holy and homely, were seen to be interwoven:
and a little oil from the lamp, blessed by an elder, could
mysteriously be used by the Creator Spirit for the healing
of his creature of flesh and blood.

The anointing of the sick today is a pale remnant of this
Catholic thinking. The risk of reinstating a sacrament of
anointing, divorced from the familiar therapeutics of today,
is the risk of irrelevance and magic. The restoration of such
a sacrament to everyday use in the Church today will accomplish little unless it is symbolic of, and accompanied
by, a very much deeper insight into the sacramental nature
of all created things, including those things which God has
given man the power to make. 'For the earth is the Lord's
and everything in it',[2] not only natural herbs but manu-
factured penicillin.

In the West today water comes to us from taps, and
bread ready sliced in hygienic wrappers. Olive oil, though
still used both in hospitals and for the Coronation at West-
minster, is less and less related to either consecration or
healing in the mind of twentieth-century man. For us the
symbols of healing are man-made—stethoscopes, syringes
and chromium-plated machines. If it is desirable for a bishop

[1] *Liturgy and Worship*, ed. W. K. Lowther Clarke, p. 477.
[2] I Cor. 10.26.

to bless oil for healing purposes on Maundy Thursday, is it not equally desirable for him to visit the hospital dispensary and operating theatre on St Luke's Day, to bless the medicines and the surgical instruments which God has given man the power to create? But would such blessing be any better understood than the blessing of olive oil is understood, unless it was a visible part of the Church's awareness of the living God at work in the hospital today? It is not yet beyond our memories that priests blessed guns and tanks in recent wars. This has devalued the meaning of blessing. But somehow penicillin, scalpel and hypodermic syringe must be gathered within the ministry of Christ's hand stretched out to heal.

Because a loaf was broken and shared, God's good purpose for all bread was revealed. Because in the history of the Church olive oil has been blessed and used, all medicines should be declared openly as gifts of God, to be used in accord with his purpose of compassion. Penicillin blessed by a bishop would be no more effective against staphylococci than unblessed penicillin, which is enormously effective anyway. A blessing is not magical. But a blessing of the hospital dispensary and theatre would call men to use them responsibly as part of God's world. It would be a natural ceremony, closely linked in thought to a Rogationtide blessing of the crops and fishing fleet. Perhaps the bottle of *oleum olivae* could be removed from the dispensary shelf and put on the table—for special blessing as a sacrament of the whole; and some of the oil then set aside for use in the anointing of the sick in the coming year. Understood this way, there would be nothing incongruous in anointing the hands of a surgeon or his scalpel at the same time as his patient.

The Christian does not enter the ward or the dispensary with the air of one who has come to announce that he has brought God. The Christian's message is 'He is here'. The anointing of a sick person in a hospital ward today so often suggests that something 'spiritual' is brought in, which can then be taken out again (and now the real business of the ward can be resumed). We need to open men's eyes to the meaning of what is there in the ward; to the way in which God, who is the source of all life and healing, gives knowledge and skill to the doctors and nurses in order to set us free.

SIN AND FORGIVENESS

The word 'sin' is used in two senses. First, it is a general term to describe the present condition of the world, and of ourselves in particular; it is the predicament of human beings estranged from God, from the creation and from one another. Creation is spoilt : man is bent. And all that comes short of the glory of God, that is' deprived of the divine splendour',[1] is sin. It is our condition on this earth. It is the tragic element that runs right through life. We are not personally responsible for it, we are born into it (original sin). We do not start life with a clean slate, but already stamped with traits of personality, racial and family characteristics.

Secondly, the word 'sin' is used to denote a fault for which we are morally responsible, such as the anti-social sin of theft. A sin in this sense has its roots in our sinful condition as described above, and is symptomatic of our underlying estrangement from God, from one another and from ourselves.

It is not uncommonly said today that disease is due to sin. In the sense of falling short of the glory of God the statement is true. In the sense of a sin as a fault for which we are morally responsible, the statement is false. Therefore some discussion of sin and its relationship to disease is necessary.

[1] Rom. 3.23.

42

The tragic and moral aspects of sin are interwoven in many sickness situations. For example, we may be tempted to condemn an alcoholic for his behaviour, and to blame him severely as we see him degenerate in character, dragging his wife and family with him into poverty and degradation. Yet the more we know of such men and women personally, the more we find how addiction is rooted in personal difficulties, often arising from a broken home background, often an alcoholic home. When it comes to responsibility, one dare not judge. There is certainly moral responsibility there: we know this is wrong: it is sin. To overcome it, there will need to be effort and decision and often this is only effective when a man reaches bedrock and knows that he cannot help himself. Yet behind the presenting symptom is a problem personality, and in a sense it is all due to his tragic background. In all this, personal responsibility must be upheld. A lively conscience, the ability to distinguish between right and wrong, and the desire to do right, are things distinctive of human dignity; they distinguish us from animals. It is only when the alcoholic accepts responsibility for himself, and acknowledges his need of help, that his addiction may be overcome.

It is not uncommon to find pastors who recognize only the element of responsibility in sin. Then instead of setting men and women free, as Jesus did, they add a burden of guilt to the sick man by moral condemnation of his symptoms, and by firmly pushing the lid back on his inner conflict. But the element of tragedy is real, and we must recognize sin as a condition of our unconscious nature which calls for forgiveness, not merely of symptoms, but of ourselves as we are. The tragic and moral elements are interwoven in ways we cannot always know. Guilt and calamity cannot be balanced against one another. Disease is not usually due to sin (in the sense of moral wrong): this is a basic concept in healing the sick. We may feel that the wicked should be sick and the good healthy : but it is not so in the world as we know it.

Nevertheless, forgiveness of sin is an important part of the healing ministry, not because the sick man is sick through his own fault, but as a step in reconciliation to God and neighbour and self. It is important in any crisis to remove the hindrances which blunt our awareness of what God is doing or which hinder God's work in us. In this regard the minister, as much as his patient, stands in need of forgiveness.

In Western society today, men do not feel the need of God's forgiveness as did the Jews in the time of Jesus. But we do experience separation from one another : we are very conscious of loneliness and the break-up of community. The concern of the Church with love and with community is an attempt to answer this isolation which men feel. Only later does a man come to see that what separates him from his neighbour is what separates him from himself : by failing to come to terms with his own anxiety or hostility he projects it upon his neighbour.

Both John the Baptist and Jesus began their ministry with the call 'Repent'. This meets with no response from man today. But to say to a man, aware of his isolation in a way that he is not aware of sin, 'you belong'—is to say something which he understands. 'You belong to us : here is a family in which you are accepted.' But we find it painful to accept ourselves, and much of what we are is held down in our unconsciousness. We are fearful of rejection, and therefore it is only within a loving relationship that awareness of what we might become can grow. But men may reject love, too.

For many today the most vivid experience of forgiveness is in work with small groups. To return to the example of an alcoholic : it is in groups of Alcoholics Anonymous that he is known as he is and accepted. Mutual forgiveness is at work. Similarly in group therapy, doctors and patients who are willing to face exposure and to be known experience that forgiveness not only of symptoms, but of themselves as they are.

The Church is healing through forgiveness today in groups of Christians, men and women, who are ready to say to the broken and isolated 'you belong': and not only to pay the cost of a continuing relationship with others in terms of time and thought and care, but also to suffer at their hands the hostility and rejection which those we love pour upon us. Love draws out evil, suffers it and triumphs over it. In such a group all are sinners, all are estranged: it is not 'I' over against 'them' but 'we'. In our common humanity, with which Jesus identifies himself, we share a common tragedy and triumph, for no man is an island. We share in one another's dying to old and childish attitudes: and in one another's rising to new maturity. And the word 'forgiveness' is one way of describing the willingness to pay the cost of continuing association with another man. God has shown us, in Jesus, his own willingness to pay the cost of such association with all men—to the loss of his reputation at the hands of publicans and sinners, to the cost of his life.

Such groups are not widely available in the Church as we know it today. But in so far as we do not do this healing work through forgiveness, we are not being the Church.

RECONCILIATION

When working in West Africa, I used to encounter men returning home from Britain. They had left us as students, Christians, young in years and experience, to study medicine, nursing, engineering, commerce, law and a host of other subjects. They came back to us full grown in manhood, confident in the strength of their experience, but often disillusioned with the Church. Common to them all was the experience of colour prejudice in Britain. For some it had meant the closed door when seeking accommodation. For others the impossibility of finding work commensurate with their qualifications. For many, the rejection occurred within a church or university itself.

In general this experience was digested and left no obvious resentment: but deep within the Negro heart was felt a resulting diminishment of human stature which has undoubtedly found outward expression in the fierce flames of African nationalism. Among the returning men one also saw those into whose soul the iron had entered. Bitterly truculent towards Europeans, they projected all relevant and irrelevant hatreds and frustrations of life upon those with white skins.

But it is not only those who receive prejudice who are twisted by it. It is those who hate. Hardness of heart, destruction of liberty, perversion of justice, these are the terrible harvest of the human soul which is closed against a brother. Similarly, the cost of racial *apartheid* in South Africa defies estimate in terms of broken lives and smouldering hatred. All of us meet the equivalent of the Berlin Wall in our own hearts. Man's own personal conflicts, writ large, face us on an international scale having acquired an impersonal power of their own to bind and twist the souls of men.

The cost of estrangement in family life is visible in the effects on the children. A broken relationship between husband and wife—whether they are actually separate or not—affects the security if not the mental health of their children. The teacher at school can often pick out, in a class, the 'problem children' (already they are labelled) from broken homes. Within their emotional life there may be sown the future seeds of further broken marriages, delinquency, vagrancy, mental breakdown or anxiety.

The Church is called to a ministry of reconciliation which involves breaking down such impersonal problems as 'race' or 'delinquency' into people. There is, first, a preventive task. By the quality of its life-together the Church has the power to reconcile men across racial and other barriers. Joost de Blank at his enthronement service in Cape Town said: 'I suffer from an incurable disease: I am colour blind.' And Alec Fraser of Achimota said: 'I have yet to meet the man for whom Christ did not die.'

Secondly, it is a task of healing the wounds which hatred and prejudice have inflicted on people in mind and heart. We have spoken above of this work in the church-community and in groups of Christians. Reconciliation—the foremost task which the Lambeth Conference gave to the Anglican Communion in 1958—is a work which has power to heal, not only relationships, but also broken hearts, minds and bodies.

In the Church of today we are faced with denominational divisions which greatly weaken our power to reconcile different races. So the Church is broken. But her ministry of reconciliation is even now going on in East Harlem and Notting Hill, just as when Paul wrote to admonish the Corinthians for their party factions,[1] the work of reconciling Jew and Gentile, master and slave, was continuing. The world is in the Church dividing Christians from one another; but the Church is also in the world, suffering, healing and reconciling men to each other.

COUNSELLING[2]

Listening is healing. A Marriage Guidance Counsellor told

[1] I Cor. 1.10ff.
[2] See W. H. Kyle, *Healing through Counselling* (1964), for a detailed description of how the Highgate Counselling Service has put into practice much of what has been written about the Church as a caring community.

me once how a young married woman came to her with a difficulty. She sat down and talked and talked without stopping. Her counsellor, listening, only put in the occasional 'Yes' and 'I see'. At the end of a long interview, the young woman got up and thanked her most sincerely for her advice! In fact no advice had been given.

To listen patiently as someone strives to put their difficulties into words: to accept without flinching a shameful disclosure: to withhold from the dangerous hobby of rushing in with our own ready-made answers: this is to enable someone to struggle through difficulties to new life and new vision. We act as catalysts in helping them to see their own problems clearly and to make their own decisions. Only thus can we help people to maturity. We are to avoid the easy alternative of running people's lives for them. We must care more for people than principles, by being sensitive to the personal needs of each person in their own particular situation or relationships: rather than applying laws by rule of thumb. We can only understand a man's actions when we know *him*.

Of course the skill and knowledge of a trained and experienced counsellor or of a psychiatrist has its rightful place and value. It is only recently that the whole field of 'Clinical Theology' has been opened up in Britain, although long studied and practised in America. Increasingly it will become a recognized part of the training of priests and ministers for their pastoral work. The study of some psychology is obviously a basic discipline for all professions dealing with people. Its omission from the training of ministers is serious, and undermines the status of the minister as pastor in the eyes of other professions dealing with people.

Here I am more concerned with describing the basic attitude of mind which underlies the pastoral relationship, whether between priest and patient, doctor and patient, or probation officer and client. This attitude of mind is some-

times described as 'non-judgemental'. It is unfortunate that
the word 'judgement' is understood to mean 'condemnation', by a strong association with punishment in the courts.
But this is only one field in which the word is used. It is used
in science and art quite apart from moral decisions. It also
describes the acts of a physician who is wise in clinical
judgement. A man may be a good judge of horses. And in
moral decisions it is just as much a judgement to say 'he is
a good boy', as 'he is a bad boy'. The pastor is neither to
condemn, nor to condone. His first act is to lay himself open
to listen : then to speak and act in love. Love of its nature
is not 'neutral', but discerns right from wrong. *Discernment*,
one of the gifts of the spirit, may be a better word than
judgement, for it carries the sense of sifting and choice without condemnation which the New Testament means by
judgement.

A great truth to be found in pastoral work is that personal
relationship itself, being a means of expressing the love of
God, can be healing. A district nurse once remarked to me :
'I went to my vicar and told him my problem; but he was so
busy listening to what I was saying and thinking out the
answer that he never listened to *me*.' This is a profound
remark. For we must not merely listen to what a person
says, but also listen to them as people; sensing perhaps the
unspoken problem, and paying attention to trivialities
which mask the *crie de coeur*.

A listener is something which we may become through
prayer; it is something which is true of us as a person. If
we are not a listener to the family at home, we shall not be
able to switch it on specially for an interview as a 'counsellor'. Listening in fact is not just a matter of keeping the
mouth shut and ears open : it partakes of the nature of love.

There are of course points in technique. For example, it
is important for a listener to sit still : not to face his patient
directly, but to sit at right angles to him : and even the

arrangement of the room may be conducive to confidential conversation or not. And discretion is vital. If it is known that what goes to a certain minister also goes to his wife, then of course quite automatically there are a lot of things which will never come to that minister. A reputation for discretion may take years to build up; and can be lost overnight. But technique alone is not enough. Only when we offer ourselves as agents for God can his strength, healing, guiding, be transmitted through the personal meeting. Father Congreve wrote: 'You do not feel that you can help anyone? Keep your own hold upon God, and you are all the help they want.'[1]

PREACHING THE WORD

When introducing the speaker to a men's meeting in the north of England, the chairman, a local vicar, said: 'I have never practised the ministry of healing, and know nothing about it; so I am particularly interested in what our speaker has to tell us.' This is a perfect opening for a speaker on the subject: for no priest can stand in the pulpit and minister the living word of God to his people, without the possibility of healing somebody in his congregation.

The crowds of Capernaum noted that the words of Jesus 'had the note of authority'.[2] The lords of storm, confusion and sickness obeyed him. And when the crowds remarked of Jesus 'All that he does, he does well,'[3] the phrase intentionally echoes the words of Genesis, 'God saw everything that he had made, and behold, it was very good',[4] for the evangelist saw in Jesus 'one who spake and it was done'.

Today the living word of God still has power to change men's lives, habits, and even their minds and bodies. We never know just what the Holy Spirit will accomplish

[1] M. V. Woodgate, *Father Congreve of Cowley* (1956), p. 33.
[2] Luke 4.32.   [3] Mark 7.37.   [4] Gen. 1.31.

through his spoken word, when received by a hearer whose heart he has prepared. One member of the congregation who hears the word of God may come to know in his heart the relief of forgiveness: and he goes home rejoicing, with a burden of guilt lifted from his back. We know how destructive of health and sanity guilt can be. Another, through the word spoken and heard, comes to know a little more of what it means to love his neighbour as himself, and returns home to make up a long-standing quarrel with his brother. A broken relationship, with all its destructive consequences, has been healed—and perhaps two men's health saved. Another through hearing the word spoken finds, perhaps to his surprise, that a chronic pain is eased and does not return. Another finds himself moved to turn to our Lord and say 'Yes' to the call which he hears: and he is changed (born again, saved, converted—whatever your language may be). Such an experience may alter a man's whole outlook, habits, or personality pattern, with wholesome effects upon his life and relationships.

The word may be read or heard in Scripture, spoken in the publicity of a pulpit or the privacy of a room. And not only a professional minister, but the lips of a friend or stranger may sometimes carry the right word in home or street or bus queue. The word of witness to Christ as Saviour may always initiate a work of healing.

There is an important field for prophecy among doctors, nurses and professions associated with medicine. These men and women are engaged in the conquest of disease. Their whole endeavour is in co-operation with the purpose of God, and this needs to be brought to consciousness, so that God may be recognized at work in and through them. So many doctors and nurses become new beings through sharing in the life of Christ, giving to their work new purpose and deeper love. The Church cares for both healthy and sick. Therefore work amongst the healing professions is an integral part of the healing ministry, which does bring together the work of faith and the work of science—sometimes in tension, but at least together.

The work of a hospital chaplain in this regard is not only as an individual pastor to the sick, but also as disturber, prophet, and counsellor to busy professional people. Although they may not see the relevance of the Church, the hospital staff are men and women peculiarly exposed as part of their daily work to the realities of death, failure and tragedy. In these conditions, carefully chosen words have power to heal or hurt, to disturb complacency and to change lives.

SOCIAL CONCERN

Much of Jesus's work of curing the sick left the root causes of disease untouched. Did the lepers whom he cured return to the homes and families where they had become infected? But his teaching has slowly penetrated the life of the world and confronts all the manifestations and symptoms of evil in whatever way they present—sickness among them.

In the hospital where I worked in West Africa there were three big problems: malnutrition, venereal disease and tuberculosis. Only too often these could be traced to the underlying social problems of migrant labour. African men left their homes and families in the North to work for poor wages on contract jobs in the South. They lived in overcrowded strangers' quarters in the towns, ate food often unfamiliar but always too starchy, and went with prostitutes. The employers took little responsibility for the wellbeing of their casual labour beyond the pay parade.

However important it is to deal with each individual in his sickness, yet basically the evils of migrant labour arise from an un-Christian view of man: man regarded as a 'thing' (as a 'hand') which works for you on the cheap. The book *Blanket Boy's Moon*[1] deals with this same problem in South Africa in a heart-searching way. The true healing ministry of the Church here lies in the political field, proclaiming the world of labour as part of God's world, and the labourer as a child of God entitled to the respect due to human dignity, with rights to a fair wage, housing and family life. Indeed the axe must be laid to the root of the tree: and the proclamation of the Kingdom of God and his justice brings healing in its wake—how could it be otherwise? To follow in the footsteps of Amos the prophet of righteousness is to expose the social sin at the root of much sickness.

In a parish in Lancashire where I worked, many of the sick whom we visited and for whom we prayed were suffering from chronic bronchitis and cardiac failure due to the breathing of industrial smoke and coughing over many years. This is the third greatest cause of death in Great Britain today. To minister to the individual is always important, but intercession here will lead us on to active concern over smoke pollution (the parish church quite rightly included a demonstration of this, its effects and costs in terms of health, in a Christian Home and Family Exhibition). We cannot try to thrust back upon God the action to be taken in such problems, where he has already put the answer in our hands. Would we anoint a man with chronic bronchitis, or give him laying on of hands, with any expectation of God's healing, if he *continued* to live in a dirty town? Would this not be a wrong way of co-operating with God—even of conniving with ignorance to obscure the true cause of the man's sickness, and the true remedy? Do we pray for those with lung cancer, but close our eyes to its connexion with cigarette smoking?

If we do not understand the dynamic relationship be-

[1] Lanham and Mopeli-Paulus, *Blanket Boy's Moon* (1953).

tween personal sickness and its social roots we run the risk of being quite unreal in our work of healing. The social concern of Christian Action for the homeless in London is a work which is contributing to the well-being of men and women. So is the work of St Martin-in-the-Fields among the needy and vagrants in London. If our healing work was more socially sensitive, we should become involved more often in such political and social service. For example, more Christians are needed in the work of hospital boards. Such work of local service is too often left to others, and is not seen as part of the Church's ministry of healing. William Temple wrote: 'The Church exists for those outside the Church.' It requires a lively imagination to see how the secular world of hospital, preventive and after-care services, can be leavened with Christian concern.

CHAPTER THREE

THE CHURCH IN THE WORLD
OF MEDICINE

Whatever may be the nature of the connexion between Christian theology and the origins of modern science [Dr Alan Richardson has written], it can hardly be without significance that the scientific attitude arose in a civilization which acknowledged one God, who was personal, rational and dependable, and that the most ardent and dedicated pioneers of the new scientific movement were themselves devoted students of the Bible and of Christian theology.[1]

In the close relationship between religion and science doctors have always played a great part. Yet today in medicine we see increasing secularism, especially in hospitals. This is not an isolated event, but part of the wider growth of secularization in Western civilization in all its life— commerce, industry, politics, education and the press. There is no specific remedy for this in medicine as if it were an isolated science: but if Christians are to be creative in any secular sphere of activity, we must desire the gift of prophecy to proclaim God's rule over, and his Presence within, all life. To do this in medicine will require special knowledge and understanding of medical thought and language.

I do not take the view that secularism is a revolt against God. Rather it is a particular ethos which has out-dated the traditional language and images of religion. In this new climate we have to learn anew how to speak of God in

[1] Alan Richardson, *The Bible in the Age of Science* (1961), p. 27.

meaningful terms: and how to create an imagery that captures the imagination and harnesses the will to the purposes of the living God who is King in the secular world. It is his world and he loves it.

Because of our lack of awareness of God at work among men in the technological world of medicine and nursing, we imagine that he is absent, and must be found in more 'religious' ways of healing. The prevalence of spiritualism, 'Christian Science', psychic and 'spiritual' healing, is in part an irrational protest against the often cold and detached attitude of doctors; and in part arises from our own lack of awareness of the living God.

Before we examine this situation further we must first see how the discoveries of science have radically changed the working partnership between God and man in the work of healing: and what the Christian contribution is to this new situation.

SCIENCE AND THE WILL OF GOD

As science advances our knowledge, we are led to meet God and to discover his will in different ways from our ancestors. Man is at last beginning to master his environment. We have eradicated malaria from Cyprus; navigated under the Polar Ice cap; sent men into orbit round the earth, and a rocket round the moon.

The fruits of the scientific method are available to us daily in our lives: preserved food, penicillin, transport, contraceptives. In the old days man was in the hands of nature: in medicine, in agriculture, and in family life he was guided by nature. He found God's will in the course of nature: for him it was the finger of God, and he reverenced God as Creator. But now we have increasing control over nature: the scientist's life is given to the mastery of nature. The Genesis stories suggest that this is the purpose of God, for man was told: 'Be fruitful and multiply, and fill the earth and subdue it; and have dominion over the fish of the sea and over the birds of the air and over every living thing that moves upon the earth.'[1]

But how is God's will to be discovered today? God meets us, I believe, at a different point. For example, in planning a family, our ancestors accepted that God sends children, and submitted to the course of nature as the hand of God. Today we can choose whether to have children or not, and how many and when to have them. God meets us at a different point. We have been given dominion over the planning of a family: and God's will is to be found in the responsible use of our knowledge about fertility and conception, as well as in the responsible use or not of contraceptives. God has given to man the power to create: he is a maker, made in the image of his Maker.

We may not put the clock back—indeed we cannot: for to try to do so is merely to make a choice which is a particular refusal to co-operate with God in the present situation. Our ancestors found God's will in co-operating with nature. We find his will today in new and strange ways, in the acceptance or rejection of responsible dominion over nature.

This governs our attitude to disease and our use of science in cures. In a case of lobar pneumonia, our ancestors (rightly) discovered God's will in the course of nature and prayed and nursed for the coming of the crisis, when with a sudden sweat and drop in temperature the patient would (about the sixth day) slip into safety and convalescence. Today we meet God at a different point—antibiotics, to use or not, when and how. For we have control over lobar pneumonia; and after giving penicillin the crisis comes within a few hours. It is predictable, swift, and a cause for thanksgiving: not anxiously awaited, slow and a cause for

[1] Gen. 1.28.

fervent intercession. Again we cannot put the clock back
God's will is to be discovered in responsible use of a new
discovery.

This does point us to the need for thanksgiving in the
healing work of the Church. If we could look at an intercession list of fifty years ago we could not fail to see how
many diseases which concerned Christians then we now
rarely have to pray about. Do we only pray about the problems which science has not solved? Our intercession lists
might suggest so. Then what shall we be praying about
when the cures for schizophrenia and cancer are given to
us?

Are we treating God as a 'God of the gaps', who is only
approached over the 'incurables'? Science does not drive
God from corner to corner in this way. It is simply that
with each new discovery, God meets us in a new way about
it. Science does not win ground from God. He remains there
all the time, and he is to be found within all these discoveries in a new way: to be spoken of in a new language
by the men who seek his ways.

Man has always been called to co-operate with God as
Creator and as Re-creator of health. Today the tools of
creation and re-creation put into the hands of man by God
are far more complex than ever before. The adze has been
replaced by the mechanical plough; the sickle by the com-
bine harvester; the leech by the hypodermic syringe; and
the village by the metropolis. Instead of interceding for the
cure of pneumonia, we must learn to give thanks for antibiotics: and pray that those who use them will do so
responsibly towards God, and skilfully and lovingly towards men. Thus we shall bring glory for these gifts to him
alone.

SCIENCE HAS A PROPER AUTONOMY OF ITS OWN:
THE CHRISTIAN CONTRIBUTION

Medicine, surgery and nursing are works of cure in their own right: they are successful, whether undertaken by Christians or not. The removal of an inflamed appendix is a technical procedure which can save a man's life, whether the surgeon is a Christian, a Moslem or an atheist. The criterion of faith is not applicable to such an operation: the only criterion is competence. And no amount of religion can be a substitute for ignorance.

Yet because God, as he has shown himself in Jesus, is the restorer of health, curing work of all kinds is an act of co-operation with God: it is in accord with his continuing work of re-creation. It is 'natural' for the body to heal, for God has put a natural healing system in the body. The great art of medicine and surgery is to discover these built-in laws of God in human nature, and to co-operate with them. For example, the surgeon stitches the skin edges of a wound together in a certain way, because he knows that like that they will heal together. And man, the lord of nature, also exercises his responsibility as creator and re-creator. The surgeon does not always submit to the natural laws of the healing of the skin. He may take skin from a man's abdomen and by skilled grafting cover an area of the face damaged by a petrol burn: this is a most 'unnatural' procedure.

The good doctor, then, is one who co-operates with God both naturally and creatively. This, however, does not make him a 'Christian': this term is reserved for men who have a particular loyalty to Jesus Christ. But it gives dignity to the work of the doctor: and his work is in no way devalued because he is not a 'Christian'.

So far we have considered medicine as a simple kind of co-operation with God: a way of co-operation which is followed by both Christians, humanists and others for many different reasons. Technical competence is essential, and the Christian is not excused from acquiring it. Lack of professional skill in a Christian doctor is not only a bad witness to his Lord and Master, but also to his medical school. Efficiency is one of the ways in which we express our charity. To give an injection with a blunt needle is not only inefficient but uncharitable. Sooner or later inefficiency and muddle hurt people.

In addition to professional competence, the spirit of service for others is also common to both Christians and non-Christians. Willingness to 'go the extra mile', readiness in a nurse to sweep a floor because the domestic staff are off duty; this would not necessarily distinguish a Christian, for there is real self-giving in the professions associated with medicine. But absence of these characteristics would be a defect of discipleship in a Christian.

In personal relationships also there is a Christian attitude to patients and colleagues which is also shared by many non-Christians. All men are children of God, with a uniqueness and worth to be respected. It is almost a *cliché* to speak of treating patients as people, nevertheless it is in his personal encounter with a patient before and after operation that confidence in a surgeon, for example, is established or not; that the subtle but all-important 'will to get well' is implanted and strengthened or stifled. Are the operation and stay in hospital seen as part of a long process of rehabilitation into life, which involves a team of men and women both inside and outside the hospital, inside and outside the church-community—or is treatment as mechanical a transaction as getting chocolate from a slot machine? Does the joy of recovery bring glory to God, or is it just another feather in the big man's cap?

What a surgeon is in himself as a man, and the way he relates to his patients, may make all the difference between slow or quick recovery, and sometimes life and death. For a patient may refuse a vital operation if the surgeon fails to win his confidence. This doctor–patient relationship was described in the British Medical Association Report as 'a mysterious and little understood element in medical work'.[1]

Therefore, although a surgical operation or an injection of penicillin are techniques in their own right, yet medicine, nursing and surgery are set in a *milieu* of personal relationships, because patients and colleagues are people not robots. There is no escape from the influence of relationship: for a person to be impersonal is merely to relate to patients in a particular, possibly destructive, way. To tell or not to tell the truth to a patient involves (among other considerations) our whole attitude to people, and whether we treat them with full human dignity or not.

I have used the surgeon deliberately as an example because his skill is predominantly diagnostic and technical: yet personal relationship plays its part. In other spheres of medical work, for example in psychiatry, the personal relationship is paramount. The art of listening, acceptance, forgiveness, and suffering with a patient play a prominent part in psychotherapy: but of course competent technique is also required.

In personal relationship also, therefore, we see a Christian way of treating other people, although this attitude is not confined (though it probably owes its existence) to specifically Christian discipleship.

It is when we turn to prophecy—the recognition of the living God at work now, in people, in their relationships, in the making of a hospital or a neuro-surgical team—that we recognize a distinctively Christian contribution, not shared by non-Christians. The Christian sees medical work in terms

[1] BMA, *Divine Healing and Co-operation between Doctors and Clergy* (1956), para. 32.

61

of the purpose of God : and therefore sees health as sub-serving the purpose of life.

There is a sense in which the doctor always loses in the long run. He must do so, because death comes to all of us. And the Christian has, perhaps, his most distinctive contribution to make in the face of this fact. For, although death casts its shadow before, sickness is not a cause for despair because the living God is to be known and obeyed and loved in situations of sickness as well as health. The Christian is one who daily discovers the secret of the seed dying in the earth in order that life may be renewed. Our service of initiation reminds us of the constant dying to the old life of self-centredness which is needed if we are to rise to a new life of self-giving. The Christian is one who approaches death, if not without human fear, yet with confidence as one who has already done his essential dying, and can with confidence and tranquillity comfort those who face death or bereavement.

One more distinctively Christian contribution to medicine is in doing the task to which God calls us at this particular time, in this particular place. In Britain there is a shortage of midwives and mental nurses. In Africa there is a shortage of all medical personnel and facilities. The Christian must be open to the need of the moment.

The task of the Church's ministry of healing is therefore *not* to create a religious alternative to science, but to recognize God at work today, revealing himself in every new discovery. Truth does not change : but our apprehension of truth and the forms in which we recognize truth change from time to time and place to place.

Once again the Christian task is seen to be, *not* to withdraw Christians from the hurly-burly of general practice in the National Health Service, but to try to train more men and women to become open to the Holy Spirit, so that they may be agents of his work in the jobs where they are; continuing to work in the modern world which with all its defects and tragedies is still the world for which God gives his Son. Christian disciples are called to work like leaven in the secular world, making their contribution in professional competence, faithful service of neighbour, in relationships with colleagues and patients, in recognition of the living God at work today, in helping men to conquer the fear of death; and in recognizing the task to which God calls us now.

The task of reconciling medical practice with the work of the Church reminds me of those adhesives used in industry and the home, where you take two tubes and squeeze together the adhesive from one, and the hardener from another. The resulting mixture sets hard. Both tubes apparently so separate, only find their meaning in relationship to one another when mixed. Separate they do not stick : together they form glue which is effective for the job. So, in a sense, do medicine and the Christian faith belong. Medicine needs the Christian faith to discover its true orientation and power. Christian faith needs areas of human life and endeavour within which to work.

We cannot always tell a Christian from a non-Christian by just looking at him. Most of what it means to live in the world and at the same time to remain in the Body of Christ, the visible Church, is hidden. But just as the scientist turns from the consideration of the universe, which he measures in light-years, to the microscopic universe of particles of energy within an atom : so the Christian turns from the worship of a God who forged the rings of Saturn, who is ineffable, over all and above all, to find him within all the homely wonders of his daily work. Work which may otherwise remain merely technical, detached and cold, becomes thereby also personal, purposeful and warm, directed in obedience and devotion to him who lay down his life for his friends.

THE DIVORCE BETWEEN MEDICINE AND RELIGION[1]

1. *From the Church's point of view*

Because of the ready availability of medical treatment in this country, the full significance of the separation between church and hospital is not realized. But what escapes notice here is plainly visible in the Church overseas. For example, in Ghana, a territory where mission hospitals have been sparse, a missionary church sets out to proclaim the good news of the kingdom of God in an African village: a Christian community grows up and becomes established. One of the converts then falls sick, or perhaps a young Christian wife finds that no baby is coming although they were married in church two years ago. What will the one in need do? For there is no hospital just round the corner.

One of three courses is likely. Either a long journey by lorry to something called 'The Government Hospital' where white man's medicine is dispensed: or a visit to the local medicine man: or a visit to one of the shrines in the forest —discreetly far from the local church. In Africa because religion and medicine are not divorced, the young convert will find himself undergoing religious ceremonies as part of his treatment. If he has chosen the Government Hospital, he will have encountered a powerful secular influence which is slowly destroying Africa's innate religious sense.

So the young convert all too easily gets one foot back in the pagan religion from which he has turned. Whether the help sought has been native medicine, or Government Hospital (or very often both), there has been exposed in his daily life a need which 'the Church' apparently did not

[1] Parts of this section appeared in *Theology*, vol. lxiii (May-June 1960), and are reprinted by kind permission of the Editor and the SPCK.

meet. In other ways, too, the Church fails to bring a Saviour who can be seen to be the Lord of the whole of life, including the African way of life. Even a Christian mission hospital may fail to preach a gospel relevant to the whole of life; for unless the hospital can be seen to be part of the life and good news of the *local* church-community, unless priest and doctor on the mission station are seen to be members of the same 'Body', then the very work of curing the sick may bring glory to Western technology, rather than glory to the Lord of Life.

A congregation may be suffering from frank signs of malnutrition, yet the gospel may seem irrelevant to the daily job of tilling the soil and growing the needed foods. At many crucial points in his life—naming ceremony, puberty rites, marriage and sickness—there are areas where the Lord of all Life is excluded. Once again secularism in medicine is seen to be one part of a wider chasm between religion and life generally.

In some parts of the world, for example in Assam, the separation of Christian healing (still supported by overseas missions) from the work of the local church (now indigenous) has become critical. A mission hospital, in order to keep up with modern advances in scientific medicine, and to comply with the high standards demanded by new Government medical and nursing services, becomes more and more dependent on money from abroad to meet soaring costs. The hospital may become a status symbol, where local Christians expect privileges over pagans. So far has the work drifted from the conception of the hospital as a local expression of Christ's compassion for all men—especially for those outside the Church.

This is not the place to discuss how such a situation can be remedied: for it is clearly a task which must take account both of the needs of the local people, in Assam or wherever it may be, in consultation with Government: and also in the context of the mission strategy of the Church in the area, planned ecumenically. We can add that in building a new Christian hospital it is essential for the local church to be involved from the outset in plans, and in the hospital governing board. Later the local church must take part in sick-visiting, welfare and after-care, sewing parties, hospitality for nurses and for patients from up-country requiring accommodation during a period of out-patient treatment, in the provision of a chaplain, in the work of healing through prayer. It is easier to begin a Christian venture in this way, than to penetrate a secular institution where attitudes to the Church and assumptions about the relation between religion and medicine have hardened.

Obviously there are areas where the Church is wide awake to these issues, and church, farm, hospital and school have grown up side by side in an ordered mission community. On the other hand Christian institutions, such as missionary hospitals and schools, are today becoming more and more of a luxury. We are called to work as Christians, scattered like leaven in Government institutions, while maintaining our membership of the Body of Christ as our source of strength and direction.

I have been concerned to illustrate the effects of the divorce between religion and medicine in their most obvious forms overseas, in order to throw light upon the hardened separation in Britain. In considering the present relation between medicine and religion in Britain it is difficult to avoid generalizations: nevertheless, they *appear* to be able to get on quite well without one another.

Conscious efforts between doctors and clergy to co-operate in general practice are spasmodic. Both are members of busy professions; but thoughtful men in both spheres of work, Christians or not, would regard some co-operation as useful. In hospitals, chaplains are often busy part-time men already heavily committed in parish work. The simple point I would make here is that where co-operation is small or absent, no one is very bothered about it, and neither doctors nor clergy feel that something vital has gone wrong with their work when both pursue their separate paths. It is left to the patient to discover the effects.

Clergy have always had a pastoral ministry to the sick, and the Church has always, since our Lord's day, cared for those in any kind of adversity. It is possible to point to periods of failure and faithlessness to her task: the persecution of the mentally sick in the seventeenth century, many of whom were executed as witches: or the 1920-1939 period when the unemployed were so rarely championed by the Church. But the healing work of our Lord as recorded in the New Testament sets his disciples a clear example. The first hospitals in Britain, and the pioneer leprosy work in West Africa, are both examples of faithful discipleship by the Church. In both these instances the value of this work has been recognized; it has become established in society and has been or is being secularized. (This is a characteristic development in other Christian work also, such as education. Both in this country and Africa, schools have first been Christian ventures, and now are being taken over by Governments. The present struggle for civil rights for Negroes in the Southern States of America, led by the Reverend Martin Luther King, will one day be history: coloured people will be first-class citizens everywhere.) The Church at any given moment seems to be called to a particular task in society: twenty-five years later, the task may be quite different. Christian hospitals and schools are naturally followed by Government hospitals and schools in which Christians work scattered among non-Christian colleagues.

If, therefore, during the first half of this century, in the field of healing, the Church has given such impetus to the treatment and prevention of rural disease in Africa and Asia, during the second half of this century we may well have to turn our attention to the casualties of metropolitan life—the mentally sick (the Church is already concerned about this in Britain), the lonely, the aged, suicides, alcoholics, drug addicts and vagrants. These problems are already foreshadowed in the cities of today, and the Church is a genuine pioneer with its Samaritans. But the 'Church's ministry of healing' is as yet too concerned with the disease patterns of yesterday.

Today many sick people regard the Church as irrelevant to their need. They turn—often quite rightly—to medicine for their cure, but often receive it without any conscious awareness of God's provision. Both the patients and those who co-operate for their cure can manage the job without 'religion'. Even Christian doctors and nurses can, with astonishing naïvety, keep their faith and their work in watertight compartments. 'Church' is thought of in terms of going-to-church-on-Sundays, Bible Classes, and other under-the-church-roof activities: while the Christian Faith is thought of in terms of moral conduct and high professional standards. Any synthesis of religion and life, or a concept of the wholeness of life, may be missing.

In the study on Christian work among nurses already referred to[1] it is suggested that a divorce between faith and work may sometimes be more an emotional than an intellectual problem.

> The discovery that a nurse belongs to a tense, narrow, exclusive Christian group, should . . . lead one to look for causes of stress in her life. Loneliness, a broken home, sheltered home life, difficulties of relationship on the ward, inability to cope with the experience of suffering and death: any or all of these may lead a girl to grasp an authoritative limited faith as the only rock in her shifting world. . . . The provision of maturing experiences—mixed conferences, work camps, seminars—has a part to play in encouraging . . . maturation in the faith. But above all, the steady effort to

[1] Op. cit., p. 27.

help a girl to digest the tough material which life serves up day by day on the ward—this is pre-eminently a pastoral task of assisting her growth. We know of none doing this better today than the tiny handful of women chaplains' assistants.

There also still lingers in the Church a tendency to retreat from the harshness of the world, with all that that implies in outlook upon the material world of bodies and bodily needs. Some of the movements within the Church concerned with the 'ministry of healing', or with social problems (for example, Christian Aid), have led the Church generally into a greater respect for human flesh and for material things as the medium of God's continuing creation. But within the Church, too, there are movements which emphasize spiritual gifts of healing, and reject medical gifts of healing. This serves to widen the gap between religion and medicine, between holy and secular.

Both medicine and religion revolt against one another's extremes, and withdraw into spiritualizing or materializing life: in both of which cases life goes bad. For religion is not something which can be 'added' to medicine. It is, for the Christian doctor, a way of life which includes his practice of medicine.

2. *From Medicine's point of view*

The continuation of the divorce between religion and medicine may be in part due to an inner religious satisfaction with the healing power of modern science and its opportunities of service to our fellow men. In a sense many doctors and nurses are 'natural' believers, co-operating with God whom they dimly acknowledge, in selfless healing work day after day. In part the divorce is due to rejection of the Church, her organizational aspect, out-dated liturgy, denominational divisions, and failure to speak in the modern idiom. Doctors (and increasingly young people in many types of work today) think inductively, whereas much

Church teaching is still (or is thought to be still) deductive.

The better-than-thou hypocrisy of so much of our church life is nauseating to thoughtful men and women, especially to the increasing number of professional people with a knowledge of psychology. The continued emphasis on the denial and suppression of 'bad' parts of the human personality in the Church's teaching and preaching seems out of date to professions who are trained to encourage awareness, openness and acceptance of the whole self. (This unresolved tension between the approach of the Church and the approach of psychology is paralleled in prison work by the conflict between punitive and educational methods in dealing with criminals. In the care of the mentally sick, educational methods have now almost prevailed.)

Whereas before the war atheism was rampant among young scientists, today science has gone far enough to bring men up against the imponderable: there is therefore a wide acknowledgement of the existence of God, although the Church has not yet been able to harvest this.

It is well to read the British Medical Association's report on *Divine Healing and Co-operation between Doctors and Clergy*, especially those sections on the religious aspects of healing (Sections 22-29) in order to understand fairly typical medical thought on this subject. Based on seventy replies to a questionnaire widely publicized among doctors in Great Britain, the report is a brave attempt to build a bridge from the medical side. The real significance of this report is that it was ever published, and in the willingness of the British Medical Association to co-operate with the Church. But behind the writing there recurs the constant image of a remote God, without whom medicine is able to proceed very nicely, but who intervenes (on request) when the doctor feels helpless. How can God, who is the very ground of our existence, be said to 'intervene' at one point rather than another in events which all proceed from his creating, not only in the beginning but in the here and now?

Among outstanding areas of human need where Church and medicine are both concerned, we may consider first the treatment of *mental disease*. New drugs and techniques available for treatment of mental sicknesses are resulting in a much more rapid turn-over in mental hospitals; but the shortage of clergy has handicapped pastoral care. I was encouraged during World Mental Health Year to find how many mental hospitals are in fact concerned about this, and how well they understood that the best hospital treatment of a mentally sick person can completely founder on the attitude of the family, his work-mates, or even his church congregation, when he tries to return to normal life again. Sheer loneliness may lead to recurrence and breakdown. Here are two halves of a task of healing minds which are not yet near enough to one another—the technical and the personal. They both belong in one common task of rehabilitation to life.

On the other hand the Church has a poor image to live down. The very suggestion that the Church could help in the rehabilitation of mental patients may bring a blistering criticism from doctors who are realistic about the situation. Too long have patients lain in mental hospital without visitors; too long have medical superintendents looked in vain for hostesses willing to have long-stay patients out for a day to their homes; too familiar is the relapse of mental patients who have been failed by local congregations. The situation may be better in America.[1]

How the technical and personal approach can be combined within a mental hospital has been described by D. V. Martin in his book *Adventure in Psychiatry*. One of the fascinating aspects of giving full play to the healing power

[1] See H. J. Clinebell Jr., *Mental Health through Christian Community* (New York 1965).

of personal relationships is the diminishing need for some of the many technical procedures, such as electric shock treatment and tranquillizers. Here is described a pioneer venture in healing where a proper synthesis between personal and technical work has been attempted. It will be a long time before the out-going ripples of the work at Claybury Hospital complete their journey.

Secondly, there are many *social problems* with which both medicine and the Church are concerned. An example is the British Medical Association report on venereal disease and young people (1964). Since 1960 the Minister of Health's Annual Reports have consistently drawn attention to the rise of venereal disease among British teenagers. With it we can join the high rate of illegitimacy, especially in London, and the growing number of girl mothers. This is a complex situation, and it is all too easy to moralize. The social, medical and religious facets of increasing sexual promiscuity are closely interwoven. But basically Western society has now abandoned Christian standards of sexual behaviour, and rejected the Christian insights on the nature of love (indeed to use the word 'love' is to risk being misunderstood) and life-long commitment to one partner as the true basis for any creative relationship. If young people are to live healthily in this situation, to discover true depths of personal relationships, and to preserve stable family life for the upbringing of their children, then there is not only a religious, but also a medical, social and educational task to be done: and the religious task is an element in all three, not something separate.

In the field of *medical ethics*, important moral decisions about life and death, brain operations that may affect personality, abortion, telling patients the truth, are made by doctors often without spiritual help or advice. The Church of England does publish study pamphlets from time to time to help doctors or nurses in training to reflect upon such very practical problems: for example, *Decisions about Life and Death* (1965). Various student bodies try to stimulate discussions; there is currently a series of lectures on these subjects in various medical schools being organized by the London Medical Group of the Student Christian Movement. But there is a vogue in the popularity of such problems, and often enough it is Christian students only, rather than the student body as a whole, who study these things together as a group. There is a place for seminar-type discussions by the student 'year' or 'class' as a whole, as a regular part of training. Wisely guided, such discussions would provide a meeting point where students with Christian faith, other faiths, or none, could together seek a deeper understanding of the issues of life and death with which the care of human beings faces all of us. In such gatherings there could be no objections on the ground of 'teaching religion': and Christians would learn humbly to listen to and to contribute to the general discussion rather than—as so often happens—merely trying 'to give the Christian answer'.

The leadership of such seminars is important. I do not feel that the leader need necessarily be a Christian. But he would need to be good at open discussion, and one who respected the opinions of others. Nor do I feel that a qualification in theology is essential: a seminar is not concerned with giving students a theologically perfect discourse which probably few are mature enough to receive: but with groping for truth together. This task should not necessarily be delegated to the chaplain. He might be the right man; or he might very definitely be the wrong man. Such seminars also need to be given at a time in the curriculum when the student has encountered the experiences under discussion. A student will work hard to solve a difficulty which he has encountered, and will only really be receptive to a seminar on 'helping the dying' when he has tried to do so and felt himself inadequate.

Perhaps we are aware, as never before, that science has not got all the answers: so if the Church has something to say, some doctors are willing to come and listen. Just because doctors are concerned day after day with human beings in need, medicine could become the bridge between science and Christianity. God is always to be seen at work in good medicine. It is not that the Church has 'got' God and can bring him to a Godless medicine, but that God is there already, and we need doctors and nurses who will act out of an awareness of his presence in them and in our hospitals. Certainly there are tasks ahead, such as the population explosion, which are unlikely to be solved by either medicine or the Church without one another. There is therefore a wide field of common concern between both professions. A secular medicine of mind and body alone cannot develop its fullest possibilities for healing men and women. We have reached the stage where medicine conceived as the science which 'restores a patient to function' is seen to be but one part of a wider task of rehabilitation to life. Function without purpose is meaningless. Many doctors are alive to these issues, and need the help and leadership of the Church.

It is becoming obvious that 'cure', while an adequate concept for much physical disease, is not an adequate concept for much mental disease. Day after day, at St. Martin-in-the-Fields in London, we see minor and major mental sickness which stems from a refusal to love or be loved. Broken relationships between men and women, parents and children, may sow the seeds of future mental stress and disease. In healing or bearing the consequences of rejection, to speak of 'love' is to use a word with both spiritual and practical meaning—like 'salvation' in the New Testament.

Priest and doctor have their own competence in the task of dealing with human brokenness—whether it manifests as 'sin' or 'sickness'. There comes a point when it is meaningless to categorize a man's distress in terms which automatically refer him to church or hospital as the suitable helping agency. Is it right, for example, that the National Health Service should shoulder the main burden of supporting people who are really just miserable?

The priest is competent in his work of declaring the purpose of God, in showing the nature of God as he is to be seen in Jesus Christ; and in helping a patient to know God and to respond to his love for him in his present predicament: the priest is also the messenger of a loving community, in-dwelt by the living Spirit of God, with a gospel of renewal of life for those in need. The Body of Christ speaks through him; breaks bread through him; lays hands upon the sick through his hands. He can move with confidence and effectiveness in his task. But because he does not know one leukaemia from another, nor a disseminated sclerosis from a subacute combined degeneration, he also moves with humility.

The doctor is competent in his scientific knowledge and technique; but even though he may regard a case as simple, yet he too moves with humility in respect of the purpose and power of God in living people. Always the doctor is aware that time is not on his side. Christ's victory on the Cross showed that love alone is imperishable; and the work of the doctor—valuable as it is—also perishes, except in so far as he contributes to the victory of love in the creation. It is one thing to restore a man to function: it is a wider and deeper task—in which both priest and doctor have their place—to make a man every whit whole.

MEDICINE AND CHRISTIANITY

Man is a unity. It is clear that doctors as scientists can say nothing about the spiritual aspect of this, but they choose to do so as Christians. The scientist is limited to a mind-body, material, concept of man (even if now expressed in seemingly non-material terms of energy): whereas the Christian thinks of man as a person—a spirit-mind-body continuum, using the word 'spirit' here to denote the non-material basis of personality which is believed to survive the death of the flesh.

To see a person whole, is to deny the possibility of dividing a man's nature into something 'spiritual' to be cared for by the priest and something 'material' to be cared for by the hospital. Although it is easier to draw the boundaries of medicine round those physical things which can be analysed and manipulated, yet the Christian contention now is that a medicine which still looks for a solution of human disease *merely* along material lines is out of date: neglect of personal and spiritual factors actually impoverishes medical work. The young man or woman who is struck by tuberculosis is not *merely* a problem in antibiotics. There are also frequently moral conflicts underlying the disease which need the help of a psychiatrist or minister.

The British Medical Association report already mentioned is correctly cautious in estimating the effects of 'spiritual ministrations' upon patients. But the Church has always sought to call out a response of faith in the sick man: a response to God's care for him. This personal response to God himself enables the facts of illness to be confronted with courage and a will to live. It enables death to be faced with hope and serenity. These are the ways of trust and acceptance through which the power of God may act in healing, endurance and personal triumph.

Medicine has its place in this; but medicine alone is not enough. Man lives by bread, but not by bread alone. There is also a recovery of the person to be made. Sometimes in spite of the best physical treatment, it is as if the patient himself has contracted out of the struggle and dies. Or on the other hand even when clinical omens are dire the patient lives by a triumph of the spirit.

Cure of sickness has its place in the total pattern of the patient's life. An operation for lung cancer may be successful, and give the patient another lease of life. But if his hospital experience merely confirms him in his life's pattern of looking after Number One, and he spends the years rescued from the hand of death making life a hell for his family, then what has been gained? A show case from the surgical point of view could be a failure from God's point of view. On the other hand, an operation which wins for the patient a scant three months of pain and weakness may yet be an experience which brings him face to face with God. The surgical failure is a success from God's point of view. And just because suffering so often crushes and does not ennoble, it is doubly important that we should not lose sight of the whole purpose of life and death, joy and sorrow.

Many doctors will deny that this has anything to do with medicine; they will say that a patient's faith and purpose in life cannot become a doctor's province. Other doctors will agree that our medical technique must subserve the purpose of enabling people to move in the direction of fulfilment in work and relationships. The old family doctor knew this well: many patients also know this well. And just so long as medicine is practised in a cold and secular way will patients continue to make their protests against this in irrational and unconscious ways by consulting 'spiritual' healers, whose techniques may be emotional or magical, but who at least give personal attention. It should be salutary for us doctors and ministers to note what a considerable number of patients in hospital have often been to some kind of 'healer'. They are looking for something which they miss in medicine—something personal, a faith and a sense of purpose and some recognition of the mystery of life and death. We all too often avoid personal relationship with

77

patients for a variety of reasons; we may feel safer pre-
scribing 'things'. But such evasion hurts people.

A Christian doctor has great opportunities to see his
patient 'whole', in his relationship not merely to his environment but also to his fellow men and to his God. And
where a doctor himself cannot encompass the whole—as
obviously he cannot because of time and opportunity, as
well as the need to make the best use of his special talents
and training—then he must see himself as one of a team
where doctor, minister, almoner, district nurse and others
do encompass the whole together: so that instead of con-
tracting out of personal demands, we act together with a
personal interest and concern which transcends barriers.
And barriers there certainly are between different professions in the work of healing. Yet the unity of the patient
needs a unified concern for his complete rehabilitation.

Where there is a genuine concern for the recovery of the
patient and his rehabilitation into life, co-operation can be
accomplished in simple ways—a word here, a contact there,
a letter or a phone call to ensure pastoral help, concerned
follow-up, the opportunity to discuss a difficulty, the support for living through a desperate situation; the counsel for
family, financial or work worries; an introduction to a lively,
caring church or minister. It will certainly not be possible
for a specialist to spend time (more valuably spent in doing
the work that only he can do) in following up details of this
kind: but he should be convinced that his own work is
partial and unfinished—if not pointless—unless he is part
of a team whose concern is for the patient's wholeness. The
practice of medicine and the rehabilitation of a patient in
life is no circumscribed skill, but a living art whose interests
and responsibilities shade off at the edges into the ramifica-
tions of a patient's daily life.

Because man is a unity, not only is medicine impoverished
by a too material approach, but the Church's work is im-

poverished by a too 'spiritual' approach. It has been well said: 'No bread, no prayer.' For in this life there is no thought of God possible without energy changes in the brain cells, whose integrity is dependent upon food, water and particular salts and vitamins. Lack of an efficient thyroid gland is sufficient to throw the whole person out of gear and render prayer impossible. Our 'spiritual life', in its Godward aspect, depends upon the adequate functioning of mind and body.

So interdependent are the material and spiritual within our nature that it should not be disconcerting to a priest when a psychiatrist clears up a guilt complex which sacramental confession failed to do. Nor to a doctor if a priest brings healing to a paralysed limb which material therapy failed to cure.

Most Christian doctors would accept that prayer can have organic effects upon the body. But any such belief is through faith alone: for there are always other explanations of such happenings which are perfectly valid in their own terms for those who do not believe in God. We cannot prove 'God' scientifically.

There is constant interaction between visible and invisible parts of our nature. In middle age a person's facial expression, the lines on their face, can tell us a lot about them because the intangible and invisible part of a person's nature shapes the face and lines upon the skin. So something invisible becomes expressed in the body, becomes 'solid' in flesh and muscle and skin—becomes 'incarnate' (in flesh). In some such way as this we think of God working to express himself in a solid creation. His love, which is invisible, becomes visible between man and man; his joy—in children; his beauty—in nature; his justice—in society; his knowledge—in scientific research; and the truth about himself—in Jesus.

In healing people we co-operate with this continuous

activity of God through knowledge and skill, through prayer and love. The unity of man's nature is a concept which governs our way of working both material and spiritual, in co-operation with the active life of God within man, within society, within history, He who is above all and over all expresses himself in all and through all.

Prayer and Work

It has been said that 'Jesus's great contribution to religion was that he did away with it'—meaning that we cannot label one department of life 'religion' and the rest 'life', for the whole of life belongs to God, and the daily living of it is a religious activity.

Unfortunately, the common use of the word 'church' to denote a building, instead of a community of living people, has made possible in people's minds a false distinction between what-goes-on-in-church and life. But just because the whole of life, including what goes on in the wards and operating theatre of a hospital, belongs to God, so too it is the Church's business. Medicine is one of the methods through which God sets men free from the things which stunt life.

In a mission hospital we can see the theatre staff stand in silence before an operation and commit their healing task to God. It is true to say that because a surgeon stands and prays with his lips he can then turn and pray with his hands. Perhaps this throws light upon the relationship between prayer and work; for certainly when we see the work of doctors and nurses in these terms, then both clergy and laity concerned with the Church's work of healing will avoid the trap of trying to create a 'spiritual' alternative on the one hand, thus leaving science to become 'secular' on the other hand. The very phrase, 'the Church's ministry of healing', may conjure up the picture of something more comfortable and pious than a session in hospital.

I have a letter from a district nurse in which she says:
'I have learnt to inject the mersalyl as a prayer.' She does
not say 'with a prayer'; for by giving the injections with a
prayer so often, she has come to see that her life as a nurse
can be a life of prayer—including the practical bits with the
hands—and so she writes 'as a prayer'. The same insight
caused Dürer to paint the gnarled hands of his labouring
friend at prayer.

Perhaps we need to see the Church's ministry of healing
in the kind of terms that an industrial Mission (e.g. in Shef-
field) sees its work in industry. In these two great fields of
human endeavour and concern we co-operate with God in
making things and in giving or restoring fullness of life to
men. In its approach to industry the Church seems to be
concerned with real issues such as just wages, housing, Sunday work, the employment of immigrants, retraining in
relation to redundancy. But in our approach to health we
seem to have withdrawn into 'churchy' activities such as
healing services. This is probably because Jesus healed the
sick; whereas there is no pattern in the New Testament for
our work in industry.

Is the New Testament to be taken as a blueprint, or as
marching orders? In the Church's ministry of healing we
have imitated our Lord's methods, rather than desiring to be
aware of how God is working in the world today. The
medical missionary movement has more truly embodied
Christ in the modern world than the Church's ministry of
healing as seen in Britain and Europe. It is not, therefore,
surprising that one of the best statements on the Church's
work of healing has been made by missionary doctors from
all over the world, met at Tübingen in 1964 under the
auspices of the World Council of Churches. They speak
from experience of the difficulties that missionary hospitals
are encountering in Africa and Asia. Faced by the widening
gap between missionary hospitals and local churches which

are fast becoming autonomous, this gathering of Christian doctors produced a statement of outstanding importance.

In particular the Consultation at Tübingen saw the role of the local congregation as a healing community, and it described the relation of medical workers to the church-community in these words:

> If healing is understood as above, it will be clear that the entire congregation has a part to play in it. By its prayer, by the love with which it surrounds each person, by the practical acts which express its concern for every man, and by the opportunities which it offers for participation in Christ's mission, the congregation is the primary agent of healing. At the heart of this healing activity lies the ministry of Word, Sacraments and prayer. The specialized work of those who have been trained in the techniques of modern medicine have their proper place and will be fruitful in the context of this whole congregational life. We have to recognize that a rift has developed between the work of those with special-ized medical training and the life of the congregation, so that often the congregation does not see how it can take a real responsibility for the work of a healing institution. One of the most urgent needs of today is that Christian congrega-tions, in collaboration with Christian medical workers, should again recognize and exercise the healing ministry which belongs properly to them.[1]

It is a decisive step in Christian thinking when a gathering of doctors from all over the world can write in this way. The work of medicine finds its true purpose within the task of the Church to proclaim God's sovereignty over the whole of life. Medical work is one part of the greater work of re-habilitation of human beings to fullness of life: a life whose meaning is to be found in loving personal relationships. Dr Lambourne has defined 'spiritual healing' as best describing 'those cases where healing results from an action done by the love of God, through the love of men and women, be-

[1] *The Healing Church* (World Council of Churches, 1965), section ii, para. 3.

cause of their love of God'.[1] This definition leaves 'spiritual healing' open to activities in the world as well as to services in church; open to doctors and nurses as well as ministers; and open to the congregation which is called to be the community which embodies the love of God in society.

[1] *Health and Healing*, the journal of the Guild of Health (January 1960), p. 5.

CHAPTER FOUR

OUR MINISTRY TO THOSE WHO SUFFER[1]

THE continuance of sin and sickness in the world is a fact of daily life as we know it. In the face of someone who has been long ill with a stubborn sickness, it is not enough to say 'God can heal you': this may be true. But we must accept the same limitations of his almightiness as God accepted in the creation of his universe. What is relevant for this sick person is what God *is* doing in this particular situation. We must keep our eyes open for the way in which God is at work in people's lives and relationships: and we see as participants, not as spectators.

God acts in different ways to change evil. It would be a mistake to limit the evidence of God's activity to the cure of disease only. God is to be sought and found in a situation of continuing sickness also. In our hearts we all know this in some measure: we are sensitive to the good and bad—the wheat and the tares—in our own selves and in others. God does not spurn us because of it: nor does it make us doubt his presence and activity in us. Man is man-in-the-making: we are not yet whole.

Today the Church has recovered her will to overcome sufferings which are destructive. The mediaeval attitude of resignation to sickness is, in the understanding of this age,

[1] I am indebted to the Guild of Health for permission to quote from a pamphlet which I wrote: *The Problem of Pain, Evil and Suffering in the World* (1962).

84

pathological. In the light of the New Testament we must make every effort to get well. It is our Christian duty. Health is something which reflects the image of God and is not to be frittered away by carelessness. Sickness, in the New Testament imagery, belongs to the kingdom of Satan and is not to be welcomed. On the other hand there are more important things than health.

We need a positive ministry to those who have resisted to the limits of their endurance and have not been cured. It has been levelled against the 'healing movement' in the Church that all we can say in the face of stubborn and continuing sickness is 'healing should have happened'. But cure is only *one* of God's answers: and when people are not cured, we can still see the finger of God at work, and help men and women in their extremity to live victoriously and bring glory to the name of God.

When we have resisted to our utmost and submitted to the working of God through every means possible, then we must accept the situation. We can let God draw us closer to himself in utter trust: we can offer our suffering for his and our creative use: and within our limitations we can continue to serve God effectively and reach out to those around us in love. Or when all ability to give has ceased through incapacity, we may have to live as faithful receivers of the ministrations of others—a far more difficult thing to do.

Pierre Teilhard de Chardin writes:

> We have come a long way, Christianly speaking, from the justly criticized notion of 'submission to the will of God' which is in danger of weakening and softening the fine steel of the human will, brandished against all the powers of darkness and diminishment . . . I can only unite myself to the will of God (as endured passively) when all my strength is spent, at the point where my activity, fully extended and striving towards betterment (understood in ordinary human terms), finds itself continually counterweighted by forces tending to halt me or overwhelm me. Unless I do everything

I can to advance or resist, I shall not find myself at the required point—I shall not submit to God as much as I might have done or as much as He wishes. If, on the contrary, I persevere courageously, I shall rejoin God across evil, deeper down than evil; I shall draw close to Him; and at that moment the optimum of my 'communion in resignation' necessarily coincides (by definition) with the maximum of fidelity to the human task.[1]

The above passage is typical of many in de Chardin's book which repay meditation. I know of no arguments for or against such a view. Either we have experienced such suffering or we have not: and in the face of those who have, we can only be humble. The point he seems to me to bring out so well is that suffering is a pilgrimage: it is our response that matters. As Edward Wilson of the Antarctic has written: 'It is not what happens to you that matters, but what you make of it.'

It is very helpful to look at the whole question of sickness in terms of 'response', rather than in terms of 'cure'. Not only to consider the patient, but also the response of all those involved in the sickness situation. Every case of sickness, or any other situation of tragedy, presents its participants with a 'learning' situation: everyone is either the better or the worse for having been involved. There are some instances where this view seems to be the only one which can make any sense out of the situation at all. For example, in the case of an elderly patient with senile dementia where the brain is affected by old age, and the 'person' degenerates into a caricature of a human being, living in the past or sunk in vegetable-like inactivity. He seems incapable of any response to love at all. Yet may not some 'meaning' be found in the response to the patient's helplessness which those who surround him make? Does this call forth *our* patience and love?

So in helping those who suffer, the first necessity is to

[1] *Le Milieu Divin* (1957), p. 73.

discover the nature of their problem and where on the pilgrimage they are; to discover what response they are making, or need to make.

The Bible does not answer the question 'why suffering?': but its different writers do suggest ways in which suffering may be met. If they do not answer the question 'why?' they do answer the question 'how?' And they answer it by describing at least six different responses:

1. *Repentance.* One of the creation stories in Genesis suggests that sorrow, labour, and evil are all man's fault.[1] It is true that sickness *may* be our own personal fault: but much more often we are not personally culpable. We all both suffer from and contribute to the social situation in which the joys and sicknesses of our day flourish (for example, stress diseases in the West). But in any tragedy, man needs to draw closer to God: confession of sin and the receiving of forgiveness helps us to be more aware of God's will and love, and to a deeper reliance on him. The pastor who ministers to the patient stands in equal need of confession and forgiveness—so do all who have the care of him.

2. *Discipline.* Every tragedy is a learning situation. This aspect of his plight is pressed upon Job by Elihu.[2] And indeed we must all know people who have been strengthened by adversity, as was Franklin Roosevelt, President of the United States. Stress in daily life is material for our learning. But we must also remember how many people are crushed by suffering: famine in the Congo is destructive, cruelty in Belsen degrading. When Zechariah says 'I will put this third into the fire . . . and test them as gold is tested',[3] one can only add: 'May God have mercy upon the two-thirds who did not come through!' Indeed we should learn from tragedy. But this is only one of our possible responses.

3. *Hope.* Hope of everlasting life first appears clearly in

[1] Gen. 3.17ff.   [2] Job 36, esp. v. 22.   [3] Zech. 13.9.

the book of Daniel, written to encourage the Jews in a time of terrible national suffering.[1] The Jews were too realistic to try to escape from life. 'This life is a vale of tears and only the future life matters' is neither a Jewish nor a Christian sentiment. On the other hand the Christian hope of the Kingdom to come in all its fullness, kindles our hope in the present to recognize gleams of the Kingdom present now. Hope looks forward, and helps us to face trouble now; to live hopefully now.

4. *Healing.* In Jesus we see revealed the thoughts of God upon sickness. He mediates the power of God over sin, estrangement and sickness. This whole book (by my deliberate choice) is devoted to *only one* of the Biblical ways of responding to evil; by healing to change the situation. It is sufficient here to note that healing is not a panacea for all tragedies. Indeed not everyone is healed, for the Kingdom of God is not yet here in all its fullness.[2] And there are other responses which the Bible suggests are suitable for those whose sickness is stubborn.

5. *Voluntary Suffering.* In the New Testament the way of the Cross refers to the life of discipleship, and to bearing the suffering which is ours by virtue of discipleship. When Bonhoeffer deliberately returned to Germany, he chose to take up a course which would involve suffering : just as Jesus set his face to go to Jerusalem. The German pastor could have remained in the United States quite honourably. But he chose to return to Germany to resist the oppression of his church, and died in one of Hitler's concentration camps. The way of purposeful suffering is a way of acceptance which grasps the tragedy of life intentionally and changes it into triumph : which takes a terrible failure like the cross and forges a mighty victory through it. It is the formidable

[1] Dan. 12.2.
[2] See J. A. T. Robinson, *On Being the Church in the World* (1960) chap. 10.

way which the second Isaiah foresaw that the suffering servant would take.

6. *Involuntary Suffering*. No one would deliberately choose to suffer disseminated sclerosis. It is one of life's tragedies, like an earthquake or sudden bereavement, which come upon us unawares, leaving us with a deep sense of the fragility of human life. How do we respond? Willingly or unwillingly? Rebelliously or with acceptance? And what's the good of it all?

In fact, *how* we suffer, may make all the difference between making or breaking us. St Paul suffered something which he recognized as evil:[1] he prayed thrice for its removal; and recognizes God's answer, not in its removal, but in the strength given to him to carry on. There is further the suggestion that this strength is not given to him to carry on *in spite of* his pain, but that it is the very weakness itself which is the rough material out of which strength is made. I have known a patient with terminal cancer, after many a sleepless night of pain, sitting up in bed first thing in the morning, answering her letters, writing to nephews and nieces, remembering her godchildren's birthdays. To the very end, she was loved and loving in the ways which progressive incapacity still permitted.

There is no single 'correct' way to respond to suffering. We must help each sufferer to find which of these responses he can make in his own situation.

To accept the situation as a discipline may enable one person to achieve new strength and refinement of personality which could not have developed but for the test of tragedy. To draw closer to God and to acknowledge our failures may result in a holiness of life which is yet contained in a broken vessel. In suffering, self-assertion may give place to humility; despair to hope founded upon faith in God. A fair-weather Christian may learn to walk by faith

[1] II Cor. 12.7ff.

89

in the dark. Another may develop endurance which can be used by God later in another sphere of life on earth. In all these trials and our response to them we can see the finger of God at work in ways that are different from cure.

Even in long sickness conditions may change: the response which has been adequate for a number of years may cease to be so. Those who have endured may recover: those who have resisted the onset of incapacity (such as blindness) may have to accept it. When faced with the alternatives of changing the situation or of accepting it, it requires great wisdom to discern the right path.

The first task, then, of those who help the suffering is the simple act of sympathy and understanding. We need to listen, to understand, to know something of the person, the circumstances, the pain and the travail. There is evidence of our Lord's own distress in such true understanding of the sufferer which precedes all work of compassion. We are not spared sweat and tears.

Through listening we participate in the patient's situation, and learn where on the map of suffering he is, and what response he is making. It is then and only then that with the greatest humility we may be able to help him along the road. We must be gentle if we wish to suggest a change of response. For we must recognize how much we can hurt people by pressing our own ready-made solutions on them. It is at least possible that we hurt as many people by pressing immediate 'healing' upon them as our forefathers did by pressing resignation. Medicine herself has begun to discover this in her own terms: it is possible to cure diseases before the lessons of the illness have been learnt by the patient.

A young girl of sixteen who develops rheumatoid arthritis needs to resist this thing which is spoiling God's handiwork. We could with confidence say that it would be wrong to welcome such sickness and to see in it the will of

God. This is to confuse evil and good. We might have to
help a person like this to a new understanding of God as he
has shown himself in Jesus, healing the sick: kindling in
her a new desire to get well. But in the kinds of real-life
problems we meet, the issues are seldom so simple.

The late Godfrey Mowat, the blind healer, was approached by certain colleagues who wished to pray to God
for the recovery of his sight. He would not let them, because the issue of light and darkness had been decided for
him already, at the time of his blinding, through prayer and
faith; and he accepted the answer from God. For in his
blindness God gave him an exceptional gift of intuition into
the hearts of those whom he could hear but could not see.
He was afraid of losing this gift. His colleagues were wrong
to attempt a doctrinaire solution and put him on a different
path, when he already knew the companionship of his Lord
upon the path of acceptance and was bringing glory to his
name.

Can we recognize that some people, on the path of
acceptance, go beyond the question of cure or not and are
transforming evil in ways which we can only guess at? Can
we face within ourselves the desire to run away from such
an idea? Even when we cannot understand this strange
work of theirs, can we go so far as to reserve judgement on
the matter? And if we meet such people who seek our help,
can we recognize that we may not be the right person to
help them?—which is such a basic truth in all our pastoral
work.

Woven and interwoven are the strands of resistance and
acceptance, of voluntary activity and involuntary submis-
sion: we do well not to dogmatize, but humbly to meet
each sufferer in his or her need, sitting where they sit, and
helping them towards a knowledge of God's love for them.

Sometimes this will take us on a desperate adventure to
the far parts of the earth in the surge of human endeavour

to conquer leprosy or malaria. We may be called to the relief of famine in India, to reconstructive work after a flood disaster, or to stay at home and cook for a widowed mother. Service is our response to the needs of people whom God puts next to us.

One person will be brought to the extremity of clinical helplessness only to find that God's love extends there also, and indeed 'healing comes from the Most High'.[1] Another person will be stayed in courage and out-going acts of love, never vanquished in heart by a slowly increasing imprisonment of weakness and incapacity until perhaps there is nothing left to offer but pain silently endured.

Each of us in our own situation has to find the living God whom Jesus has shown to us. For, when we suffer, we look not for a theory but for a person. So may Christ be found in us and in our Church by those who seek him. And may we in our need find him in the face of friend or stranger.

[1] Ecclesiasticus 38.2.

CHAPTER FIVE

WAYS FORWARD

ANY way forward begins in the mind of God, who is working out his purpose, and calls us to co-operate with him. The writers of the Bible recount what God himself has done in history, and is now doing; our task is to discern what kind of world and what kind of Church he is making. The changes in healing since the beginning of the century (even since 1945) are very great. It is this constantly *changing* world of ever increasing skill and knowledge that a flexible 'Church's ministry of healing' is called to penetrate and serve.

A. *There is no way forward for a ministry to the sick, divorced from man's predicament as a whole.*

Care for the sick will always be one sign, among many, of life stirring through the household of God as a whole. We have seen how care for people is rooted in community-life, in prayer, fellowship, and social concern for the world.

Sickness is only one symptom of man's estrangement from God, neighbour and environment. The way forward for a local congregation may not be in the formation of a prayer group for the sick, or other activity directly thought of as 'healing', but first perhaps some sign of care about its young people, the lack of Christian nurses at the local hospital, the secular teaching at a local school, the housing conditions of West Indians or the loneliness of overseas students, the latch-key child, or broken marriages. It would be wrong for a congregation in Smethwick to neglect the disease of inter-racial prejudice in order to pray for the sick : or for an industrial or suburban parish to neglect the problem of venereal disease in teenagers in order to collect money for lepers overseas. A church might do both. But priorities should be clear. The church in Birmingham must wrestle with Birmingham's problems first, while mindful of the worldwide Church.

Our concept of sickness is today based on an understanding of the wholeness of life. The sickness situation is a family and social situation in which both patient, relatives, neighbours and Health Service are involved. Although a man's immediate concern is for cure of his sickness, yet even superficial examination of him as a person must take into account his interlocked relationships, which are involved with him in health and sickness. A deeper examination may leave us in doubt as to whether he will, in the long run, be most helped by a social worker, the Marriage Guidance Council, a psychiatrist, a wise friend or his local church.

The Church has been seduced by the specializers, so that often clergy fight shy of 'the ministry of healing' as not being within their competence. Yet the Church must work for God's kingdom in the particular way and in the particular place where he has set us. If there are sick, we must visit; if naked, we must clothe; if prisoners, we must go to them; if schools, we must teach in them; if strangers, we must take them in.

B. *The Church's ministry of healing is in the world.*

We have seen repeatedly how the work of the Church for sick people needs to invade the places where in fact the sick are being cured—in hospital or home. This will usually be through those members of the Christian community who are specially trained and gifted to cure—doctors, nurses, physiotherapists and other professions associated with medicine. But suitably selected and trained sick visitors and prayer cells have their place. The minister who has a doctor or nurse in his congregation will consider their special needs; together with those other church members who work in professions dealing with people, such as probation officers, teachers, welfare workers, health visitors and many others. Discussion of common professional problems in small groups can be most useful. Work with people is exacting, and Christians are helped by training in personal relationships, in sensitivity to others, in awareness of what God is doing in the situations of daily life, as well in knowledge of the Bible and Christian faith. Christian Teamwork run such training courses for parishes, as well as training courses for men and women in the professions, commerce and industry.[1]

In discussions on the ministry of healing in various conferences, different ways forward are being canvassed: but anything which tends to separate out the Christian contribution and to develop it as a 'religious' speciality will only exacerbate the present trend towards secular medicine. For example, a 'department of spiritual therapy' has been suggested for a hospital, where patients with spiritual problems can be referred. Surely nothing—however convenient—should be done which might suggest that spiritual work can be separated out from the rest of the hospital work. Nor can the Christian faith be presented as a universal salve for the ills of mankind. Indeed the gods of peace and ease have always foundered upon the stark reality of life.

God is to be found amid the daily work of every department, and he is to be declared as Lord of all life. Let pastors be seen on the wards, and not chairbound in an annexe to the psychiatric department. And let the work of doctors and

---

[1] Christian Teamwork (Institute of Education), 1 Whitehall Place, London, S.W.1.

nurses be known as something which through Christian dedication, can be as much a vehicle of the power of the Holy Spirit as the Chaplain's work. A good Christian ward sister on each ward would soon starve the department of spiritual therapy out of a job. A readiness to listen would be one of her qualifications; and a forgiving spirit, which accepts people and maintains their sense of value as persons in the impersonal rush of a modern hospital; a willingness, too, to talk about God when asked; and a determination to keep her faith related to the life and death issues of her ward.

Much has been written by others on co-operation between doctors and clergy, usually from the point of view of complementary ministries to a patient.[1] Important though this is—it should take place as a matter of course—it is bound to be of limited scope, for both professions consist of extremely busy people.

In the last five years many groups of doctors and clergy have met in the United Kingdom. A special number of Contact[2] was devoted to the work of such groups; and a recent survey of groups at present working in Great Britain has been published by the Institute of Religion and Medicine.[3] Some of these groups have only met a few times, others regularly; but not many for more than three years. The main fruits of such meetings have been in bringing local doctors and ministers into personal touch, so that friendship may extend to co-operation over individual patients. It seems to be most valuable for the two profes-

[1] See L. D. Weatherhead, *Psychology, Religion and Healing* (1951), Section 7, chap. 2, *inter alia*. This is an authoritative book on the whole subject of the Church's work of healing; H. C. Trowell, 'Co-operation between Doctors and Clergy', *Theology*, vol. lxvii, no. 523 (January 1964), p. 3; S. Bayne, *An Address on Doctor-Clergy Relationships*, Churches' Council of Healing (Annual Report 1962).

[2] 'Doctors and Clergy Meet', *Contact*, no. 10 (April 1964), University of Edinburgh, Edinburgh, 8.

[3] M. J. F. Courtenay, *The Promotion of Field Groups* (1964).

sions to meet for an evening to study some common pastoral problems such as anxiety, guilt or stress disease. This leads indirectly to a deeper understanding and respect for one another's work. After a time groups have tended to run out of subjects. But recently the Institute of Religion and Medicine[1] has begun work with Field Groups which are open not only to doctors and clergy but also to other professions engaged in the field of healing (physiotherapists, nurses, psychiatric social workers, social welfare workers, almoners, etc.). Some groups are engaged on a common task: one is working in the London area on 'the psychological and spiritual factors underlying despair which may lead to homelessness'; and another is working on problems of stress. The Institute has a central organization with commissions on mental health, education of medical and theological students, and doctor–clergy co-operation: it was founded in 1964 and because of its wide appeal to many interrelated professions, as well as to those of Jewish, Catholic, Protestant (and perhaps other) faiths, it is opening up creative work which is long overdue in this field. The Scottish Pastoral Association[2] has pioneered this kind of work in Scotland since 1958.

Several conferences of doctors and clergy have been held in recent years. None has proved more fruitful than a working party from the two professions and many different churches called by the Churches' Council of Healing in 1961. They produced a short and most useful memorandum on the place of psychology in the training of priests and ministers.[3] Co-operation within the Methodist Society for Medical and Pastoral Psychology has for many years made training courses available for Methodist ministers. These

[1] 58A Wimpole Street, London, W.1.
[2] This Association produces *Contact*, see p. 96.
[3] Churches' Council of Healing (Annual Report 1961).

are excellent examples of the fruits of pooled experience from the two professions.

Doctor–clergy groups, extending to include other professions associated with medicine, will continue to be an important ingredient of the local healing ministry. But for practical reasons the occasions on which a doctor and minister co-operate over a patient will be comparatively few, though none the less important. In the work of the Church, co-operation between doctors and clergy is no more important than co-operation between teachers and clergy, or parents and clergy, or almoners and clergy. In respect of Christians the minister's job is to enable *all* lay believers to fulfil their own priesthood. In respect of non-Christians, the priest is a fellow-worker concerned for the welfare of those in need, with his own particular contribution to make.

Co-operation between doctors and clergy is pushed to the limit in a man who is both. There are today quite a sprinkling of priest-doctors, either working predominantly in medicine or as priests; but not often in work which combines both disciplines, except in the Church overseas. At a time when the Church is recovering a sense of her nature as a healing community, and doctors are also becoming aware that science has not got all the answers, the priest-doctor has a particular task of interpretation for the one profession to the other.

In 1962 the Church Assembly asked for the appointment of a priest-psychiatrist in every diocese of the Church of England. Although one can appreciate the value of this in the pastoral care of priests themselves, yet the appointment of priest-doctors on a large scale would be a retrograde step. The Church's task is to encourage more Christians to train as psychiatrists, and to bring more psychiatrists to a knowledge of Christ, so that they may do their work under the rule of God: and to train them, as laymen and laywomen, to *minister* to their patients. Exactly the same case could be made out for priest-probation officers, priest-almoners, priest-teachers. But with the development of professions caring for people, these ministries have been taken out of the professional priesthood and given to lay people. It would seem wrong to try to re-introduce into the professional priesthood work which has developed out of it into the priesthood of the laity.

The priest does contain within his work the seeds of other professions, for in himself he is a sacrament of the whole. Some of the seeds have grown and become independent plants, like social welfare work and psychiatry. Other seeds doubtless await the future unfolding of God's purpose. The priest's work therefore has similarities in its pastoral encounters to the work of a psychiatrist, but the priest has his own work in the healing community. This is different from the work of a psychiatrist, and indeed includes the psychiatrist himself in his cure of souls. It is the priest's work which helps a Christian psychiatrist to work and suffer in the world as a member of the church-community: as a member through whom those in distress can encounter the love of God. And if he is to continue his work as a psychiatrist, it is a pity to ordain him: unless he has a vocation to ordination, which may come to a man in any profession, but that is a different thing.

The parish priest or minister is not the right person to become totally involved in a ministry to 'the sick', because he also has the 'cure' of the healthy: whereas certain laity are involved in the ministry of healing day after day—doctors, surgeons, psychiatrists, nurses, almoners, physiotherapists, pharmacists, occupational therapists and other professions associated with medicine. Many other workers like probation officers, prison visitors, moral welfare workers, teachers and children's officers, are so involved in human problems that their work too has repercussions on the health of those with whom they deal. Some of them are

Christians and some are not, but a most impressive number are dedicated to their work of helping the sick and the broken. They are out in the world day by day. Is the priest's job to become one of them? In the occasional instance of a special calling, yes. But as a parish priest, no. His task is rather to get to know them, and, when they are members of his congregation to teach them, to train them to pray, to break bred with them and for them; to listen to the tangles which their own work ties around them, and advise them on helping others; to gather them into the Body where they are fed and fitted and trained for their work of healing, for their service to those in need; to comfort and send them out again; to hold them in his prayers; and to offer them and their work at the altar.

In his turn the priest, like other men, will receive their ministry to him. They will tend him in sickness, deliver his wife in childbirth, and immunize his children. In addition he will rely on countless Christians and non-Christians to sort out his parishioners' problems: and this dependence upon pagans for assistance with his ministry (as for his daily food and transport) is God-given.

Do not we ministers recognize that a great deal of what used to be regarded as the work of a priest has now been shared out among the professions ministering to people? Dr Fisher, when Archbishop of Canterbury, wrote:

> When it comes to dying, there is no distinction between doctor and chaplain—both are pastors and the faith of the doctor can often do far more than that of the chaplain, just because the doctor has been fighting the battle of life and death with the patient day by day more intimately than can often be the case for the chaplain.[1]

The pamphlet *Care of the Dying*, from which these words are taken, illustrates fully how a Christian doctor can *minister* to patients. In the person of a Christian doctor,

[1] C. Saunders, *Care of the Dying* (1959), p. 1.

professional competence and devotion to our Lord find united expression.

A great deal of thought has gone recently into clergy–doctor co-operation. I wish as much was going into training in personal 'ministry' and the ongoing support of nurses and other professions associated with medicine, not to mention doctors and social welfare workers. The Church is hesitant in making full use of its laity : but it is a mistake for priests to try to do what in fact Christian doctors, psychiatrists and nurses can do equally well or better.

The Church's ministry of healing is in the world, and it is laymen and laywomen who are most in touch with those who are in distress. They are at the frontier of the Church's work. Because so much medical work is secular, it is no answer to try to recover a ministry of healing centred upon the church building, or upon an ordained ministry, as if this could give us back the 'spiritual factor' that is missing. We must recover the sense of true ministry among lay people : and equip them for the Church's work where they already are—in the world.

The world that is coming into being today is distinctive (in the realm of *things*) for scientific advance : and (in the realm of *persons*) for a compulsion towards relationship between nations and between individuals. God is to be discerned at work in what is coming into being, in his gifts of discovery to men, and in compelling men to learn to live together. This calls for a new awareness among Christians of what God is actually doing today, and how he is opening men's eyes to himself. At present there is emphasis in the Church's ministry of healing on the New Testament miracles of Christ and on trying to reproduce them. Much of this work is fantasy, concerned with imposing principles on life, rather than examining the reality of life as it is. In the Church we must take medicine seriously as the work of God which he is entrusting to men.

Making and discovering things (such as medicines) is one way of working with God today. But God also acts in history: he is concerned with men and societies. We are to see him at work not only in healing bodies, but also in healing societies—in the agony of racial strife, for example, through which integration is coming into being. The recognition of the work and purpose of God in the world is the task of prophecy. May this gift be given to the Church today that we may see clearly how to work with God in ways of his choosing!

THE HOSPITAL TODAY

Today there is a need for experiments in thought and life. Most new patterns of work in the healing ministry are involving people on a local basis (for example in the street, factory or hospital), not on a congregational basis. At least three factors are common to the developments under discussion; flexibility, a search for community and interdenominational co-operation.

Dr Kraemer has written:

> One of the main effects of 'secularity' is the emergence of new world structures and social structures of high mobility . . . All religions face the same huge proposition of achieving a break with their own social past. . . . The social forms created in the past which the religions, so to speak, inhabit at present, were partly of their own making; whereas the emergent, religiously emancipated and autonomous new structures of our scientific industrial society are not. Nor do they seem to offer congenial opportunities for 'inhabitation'. Yet the inescapable task for the religions is to sow and sink themselves anew in this changed and autonomous world.[1]

This describes exactly the task facing the Church in the hospital—and therefore the task facing her ministry of

[1] H. Kraemer, *World Cultures and Religions* (1960), p. 349.

healing. Bishop Wickham has described the fruits of fifteen years of wrestling with these difficulties in industry.[1] The whole Church has learnt a great deal from this concentrated pilot scheme. We badly need a similar localized attempt to wrestle with the Church's relationship to doctors, nurses and allied professions, both in hospital and in the local health services.

The New Testament images of the church are fluid, adaptable and dynamic. There is no reason whatever why she should not penetrate the new healing world of science—indeed she must. But the Church's official 'healing ministry' as it exists today is too frozen in ecclesiastical moulds, or busy trying to prepare the way for the wind of the Spirit by a literal imitation of the biblical methods of long ago, and is diverting thought and energy very badly needed for this new task. Our church structure must yield to dictation by the needs of the world.

In hospital work we are faced not only with the ecumenical task of bridging barriers between one denomination and another, but also between different Christian societies and organizations working among nurses and medical students. Outsiders see that the Christian community is broken. Yet we are one in Christ: we do not need to create unity, our task is to express it. A greater conception of the Church's work in the hospital for the Kingdom of God could draw all Christians into one Body: and Christian witness will remain ineffective until the Christians are ready to submit their differences to Christ and acknowledge him as Reconciler. Our divisions bear witness to our distance from true commitment.

Because so many staff live out of hospital, we are most likely to make our Communion in our local church: but the practical outworking of that lies in our daily work in hospital. We make our Communion with our fellow Anglicans

[1] E. Wickham, *Church and People in an Industrial City* (1957).

or Baptists or Methodists or Catholics, but they do not work in hospital with us. The Christian colleagues with whom we work and eat and dance are not the Christians with whom we make our Communion. Up in the theatre the Presbyterian surgeon and the pagan anaesthetist, the Catholic sister and the Pentecostalist nurse, the Anglican medical student and the Methodist student nurse work smoothly as a team to save a patient's life. God is to be recognized at work through them, healing. But when it comes to co-operation on a specifically religious basis we fall apart.

At present the Christian societies in hospitals tend to produce men and women who are keen individual disciples of Christ in their personal way of life, and in high professional ideals. But there is little influence on the life of the hospital itself; for only a Christian community can wrestle with the difficulties involved.

A small group of Christians in one big teaching hospital, widely drawn from different denominations and Christian societies, as well as representative of the different professions in the hospital, including clerical and other staff, has sought to discover what it means to *be* the Christian community in a hospital. Their chaplains were co-operative, and they tried to work quietly on a threefold programme.

Silent prayer together weekly. Roman Catholics have now begun to join others at prayer, but so far do our loyalties divide us, that silence is one of the few worshipping experiences which excludes no one. A movement towards unity begins with a wordless receiving from him in whom all things shall be gathered into one. So we are united in common concern for that part of God's world where we are called to serve—the hospital.

An effort to *break down barriers* between one department and another in the hospital. Choosing just one department of the hospital in which to start, a beginning was made by meeting the staff, and trying to understand its work better. The crossing of barriers in the professional world is always costly: unbelievable obstacles exist between the mixing of senior and junior medical staff, between senior and junior nursing staff, between qualified hierarchy and students, between one profession and another. Different hours, different dining rooms, different sexes, in fact everything that could divide and fragment person from person is arrayed against community in hospitals. But there is always a first step, so long as we are prepared to begin humbly enough.

A co-operative venture to study a problem in hospital life. In a week-end conference together this group expressed concern about the way patients die in hospital. Why does one ward call in the chaplain and another ward does not? Why does one surgical team drug their terminal cases heavily and another not? Are patients told the truth? Is human dignity respected in this common human experience? They saw the need to carry out a fact-finding survey first.

We need to recover a sense of the Church being the Church-in-the-hospital with chaplains as ministers to this whole rather specialized community. In this way the Church could express a concern for the world in which the Church is called to work: it could show concern not primarily for Christian organization, but for the life of the hospital and the way patients are cared for.[1]

The position in smaller hospitals with part-time chap-

---

[1] I believe this conception of the work of the Christian community (The Church-in-the-hospital) is comparable to the 'Parish Meeting' familiar to those interested in the Parish and People Movement. In a parish, once a week, the whole congregation meet with the clergy to discuss the life of the locality, and the strategy of the Church's work there. The whole church together thus try to discern God's will for them in that place in relation to the sick, immigrants, housing, education, etc. The church-community, whether in hospital or parish, does not exist as an end in itself, but for the creation of community in the world in which God calls it into being.

lains is of course different. There are advantages—the closer relationship between a local hospital and a local church-community, for example. But also there are disadvantages —the growing number of nurses and other staff who live out and work fixed hours. Ministry to such staff, even during training, may be defeated by the practical difficulties of time-tables.

In mental hospitals there is a growing recognition of the value of open discussion between patients and staff. In addition, in some hospitals, all the ward staff, medical, nursing, and allied professions, meet regularly for group discussion as a staff. This is both group therapy, team training and fellowship—no one word quite sums up the activity. In this way, those in touch with the patients are helped to an understanding of their problems, and of their own reactions to patients and to one another. When such an accepting community is built up, personal relationships are discovered to be basic in therapy, just as they are in the sickness situation. Christians are there—the Church is there —in the midst of staff of other faiths or none : they are not called to find some religious escape, nor to talk a pious language : but to bear the burden and heat of the day with their colleagues, to show by their living and working what it means to be a Christian. As mental hospitals are closed, and rebuilt as psychiatric wings of general hospitals, so it may be that the value of this corporate experience will spread to other staff. The writing is on the wall for the hierarchical structure of hospitals.

The value of such group and on-going seminar work among those who counsel sick people or problem families is now widely accepted. It also has a valuable place in training pastors and is used in the Diploma of Pastoral Studies begun in Birmingham University's Theological Department in 1964. Edinburgh University also plans to institute a similar Diploma and Certificate Course in Pastoral Studies in the near future. The Clinical Theology Association in Nottingham has pioneered a somewhat different type of group training for pastoral work among Anglican clergy, and has flourished because of the lack of such basic training in theological colleges. Training by interview experience with people, while also participating in seminar and tutorial sessions, would seem to be vital for all men taking up pastoral work.

HOSPITAL CHAPLAINS

At present there are two different views of the hospital chaplain's work. He can be thought of primarily as a personal pastor to the sick, or as the priest to a particular kind of community which includes both sick and healthy people. It is convenient to discuss these two views separately, although they overlap: indeed the second includes the former. But to separate them will expose a certain drift in the position today of which we ought to be aware.

1. *The personal pastor to the sick.* It is the accepted view in the National Health Service that the chaplain is at the service of the sick. Although many chaplains do in fact work among the staff, yet in other hospitals chaplains have been told by the Board that the staff are not their responsibility. The present tendency to think of the ministry of healing in terms of a sacramental ministry, the laying on of hands and healing services, encourages the concept of a priestly task carried out personally to the sick. The study of 'clinical' theology can also lead to the conception of the priest's task in terms of personal counselling to sick individuals, rather than to making him a more mature minister for coping with sick and healthy. Doctor–clergy co-operation has encouraged a similar elevation of the priest's ministry to the individual sick person. All these factors seem to be working together to give us a single image of the hos-

pital chaplain as a personal pastor to the sick—*which of course he is.* There is nothing wrong in the conception : it is only inadequate when we adopt this as the only image of a hospital chaplain's work. Nor is there anything wrong with the teaching of 'clinical' theology—indeed it is indispensable for a profession dealing with people; nor with the sacramental ministry, which is vital; nor with doctor–clergy co-operation, which should be occurring quite naturally. But all these things, so good in themselves, are producing priests who are becoming specialists in personal pastoral work to the sick. An image of the priest is evolving which presents a figure who may well come to work in a white coat, standing beside the doctor, but with a cross in his lapel instead of a stethoscope in his pocket.

2. *The priest to a particular kind of community.* The truth is that the priest is a personal pastor to the sick, who recognizes in sickness a supreme opportunity for learning and for compassion, also for a contact with troubled people and their families which may be all too fleeting—*but his ministry to the healthy is equally important, and sometimes more so.*

Is there any more important part of a hospital chaplain's work than to help young nurses, who, while still immature, are thrown into an encounter with suffering and death in its most fearful forms? No wonder there are casualties among student nurses! Some of whom develop a protective shell of hardness; take to drink or drugs or sex; or leave work altogether. Others take refuge in a narrow Christian faith or sect, which at least has the virtue of certainty in an otherwise shaking world.

The hospital chaplain is priest and minister to all members of the hospital community. The problem of shortage in the ministry faces the Church in hospital as elsewhere. But the answer is not in specialization upon the sick to the neglect of the healthy from sheer inability to do both. Part of

the answer will lie in recovering a true sense of the meaning
of priesthood, and the priesthood of all believers, in this
particular field of human life and endeavour. We have
already discussed how lay men and women, ward sisters,
almoners, physiotherapists (all of whom may be in contact
with a patient more directly and personally than the chaplain) need to 'minister' to their patients. Having worked in a
hospital in Africa with both European and African staff,
my own experience of the ability of sisters and nurses to
minister to others always makes me hesitate to take on
work at which I know they excel. Our task is to train and
support them, through regular seminars on the emotional
and spiritual problems which such work involves.

In a more specialized way we are already seeing this
work as a field for women workers, selected and trained as
assistants to chaplains. Not only do they undertake pastoral
work with patients but also because of their skill, and perhaps the possession of a flat outside the hospital, they can
help nurses in personal difficulty. We shall see, in due
course, assistant chaplains working in the same way as
curates in a parish. There is room for real experiment and
thought, especially in the use of laity: so many people
today do not want the advice of a priest, but a priest's
advice can still reach them through trained laity. The King
Edward VII Hospital Fund are financing a research project
into the nature of hospital chaplaincy work at present, and
this survey is to be welcomed.

The hospital chaplain has a special responsibility for
prayer in the life of the hospital. And in celebrating the
Eucharist he will offer to God the whole life of the hospital,
ward by ward, department by department, person by person, that each and all may come between God's hammer
and his anvil, that the crooked may be made straight. From
this service his ministry to individuals and to the hospital
community at large will reach out. Wherever he goes he

stands for the Church, without whose enlivening presence the work of a hospital can become so impersonal and secular, so unrelated to life as a whole, unaware of the living God at work in their midst, insensitive to the true needs of the society which they serve. He stands too as judge, a constant rebuke to the *hubris* of science and a reminder that all our knowledge is partial. At every point of the hospital's work it is the chaplain who can help men to be aware of God himself at work in and through the every day.

As full-time chaplain, he may be able to link patients with the family life of a local church, through prayer, visiting or follow-up. As part-time chaplain he may find that many of the hospital staff who live out are his parishioners. But too often the family life of the church locally is poor and shallow. It is, for example, difficult to link up nurses, who write for a local commendation, with a lively church. And the parochial system is quite inadequate to help student nurses who move from hospital to hospital during their training.

It is in all these contacts with patients and staff that an image of the work of the priest and the Church is being built up in people's minds and hearts. Hospital chaplaincy is, therefore, one of the key points for the future of the Church's ministry of healing. The chaplain is there, at the point where hospital and church meet, where science and religion are neighbours if not colleagues. And the living God is there at work, across all the barriers which our minds erect, looking for willing hands with which to serve men and women in their need.

NEUTRAL TERRITORY

At a meeting of local doctors and clergy, one of the general practitioners put forward the following proposal.

'Often enough,' he said, 'I have a patient who needs spiritual help. If I suggest any such thing, I am met with a blank refusal to have anything to do with the clergy or church. I would like to see a house in this town, manned by a team of Christian people from different churches, chosen and trained, where I know a patient could be sent for first aid : where he would not be confronted by a dog collar, a lot of moralizing, and the possibility of being "got at"; some sort of neutral territory. I'd like the 'phone number on my desk.'

There are many places, especially in cities, where the Church is ready to care for those in trouble. The Samaritans, in an increasing number of places, undertake to meet the particular difficulties of those in despair.[1] Other churches are ready to help in a wide range of social problems. Examples in London are St Giles in Camberwell, St Botolph's in Aldgate, St Martin-in-the-Fields, the Methodist Counselling Centre in Highgate, the City Temple Clinic in Holborn : all are well known for their 'casualty work'. The Church Army, Salvation Army, and West London Mission (Methodist) are distinguished for their hostel and rescue work. Other organizations like the Cruse Club which is pioneering personal and social help for those who have been widowed, are motivated by Christian principles, but are not in any sense 'church' organizations. These examples are drawn from London because it is the city which I know best.

There are also numerous facilities in the welfare services for all kinds of personal crises; and within the welfare services are Christians capable of giving spiritual advice or of helping people to find the right source of it.

This work is admirable, yet there is still a need for local congregations to mobilize the divine and human resources required for rehabilitation, befriending, and 'standing by' those in serious trouble. It is entry points to human care and fellowship that are needed. A doctor or social worker

[1] See *The Samaritans* by their founder, the Rev. Chad Varah (1965).

may want to send a man who is lonely and withdrawn, living by himself, perhaps undergoing psychiatric treatment, and out of work, to a church or 'neutral territory', and to be sure that they will take him on and that he will not still be wandering about three months later having been dropped. I believe that spiritual casualty work must often be done within the context of supporting care of this kind. Those who work in the Church's ministry of healing are not excused the blood, sweat, toil and tears of human involvement.

For practical reasons (if not theological) this work requires to be done on an ecumenical basis. A general practitioner will have patients who belong to many different churches : it is not always easy to find a wise counsellor, or sustained friendship, for someone who is troubled or lonely. A doctor may well hesitate to ask a minister whom he does not know personally, to help. The co-operation of local churches in a counselling centre could simplify the doctor's task in obtaining help. Perhaps local Councils of Churches could undertake such work on the basis of a survey of local needs linked to existing social services.

People in distress usually require prolonged care, and many places today are pioneering residential centres where broken lives may be mended, and life resumed.

Such is Cala Sona,[1] a home in Scotland for the rehabilitation of refugees who through age or infirmity are rejected by the usual agencies. Or the Richmond Fellowship,[2] a Christian organization which has several half-way houses in and around London where patients who have been discharged from mental hospital, or people who show signs of stress or early mental breakdown, can live as a family and go out to work; thus finding their feet again before being exposed to the full hurly burly of normal life. St Martin-in-the-Fields

[1] Cala Sona, Netherton, near Wishaw, Lanarkshire.
[2] The Richmond Fellowship, 20 Argyll Road, Kensington, W.8.

has a 'House of St Martin' in Somerset where up to twelve men are taken for rehabilitation in a family unit, living and working together with Christian staff. This is linked with a half-way house in London which eases the return to life in a city.

These are but three examples of Christian adventuring in the ministry of healing; although I doubt whether any of the three would describe their work in those terms, so remote has the term 'ministry of healing' become from so much of the Church's work for the sick. Yet it is in these new patterns that we find just that necessary blend of Christian faith and care with scientific knowledge which must surely be the mark of the Church-at-work, healing in the twentieth century. It is in these kinds of terms that the Church needs to seek ways of healing the sick today—for the Good Samaritan of today does not use wine and oil for antiseptics, nor donkey for transport. He has more modern ways of expressing his compassion, and it is *that* which does not change down the centuries.

'For when I was hungry, you gave me food; when thirsty, you gave me drink; when I was a stranger you took me into your home, when naked you clothed me; when I was ill you came to my help, when in prison you visited me. . . . I tell you this: anything you did for one of my brothers here, however humble, you did for me. . . .[1]

When I telephoned Mansion House 9000, you came to me. . . .[2]

THE PASTORAL PROFESSIONS

The professions who deal with people in distress—nurses, almoners, prison visitors, probation officers, welfare workers—require special training for their work. They are experts. The poverty of training for Christian work often

[1] Matt. 25.35.
[2] The telephone number of the Samaritans in London.

compares unfavourably with the excellence of our professional training. Granted that professional competence is essential as a way of expressing our care for people, at the same time the spiritual and personal demands of any task ministering to the sick are heavy.

Many local churches now have groups who pray for the sick and troubled. But how many churches offer vocational training in prayer, the relevance of the Bible to life today, awareness of God at work in his world, personal relationships, listening and sensitivity to others, for those who are actually ministering day by day to the sick and broken, individuals and families? Christian training for these professions is required. Centres for training Christian leaders, such as Lee Abbey and Scargill in Britain, play an important part here. And those who are given a new vision of their true Christian calling—to be fully human—return to the forefront of the Christian mission in their own work. It is not surprising that many nurses, for example, avail themselves of the opportunities offered by Lee Abbey.

Christian Teamwork (sometimes together with the Tavistock Institute of Human Relations) runs courses of training for parish groups, or for those working in special fields, such as industry, social welfare, or the Church. Their training is not confined to merely intellectual knowledge, but provides experience which can result in awareness of God in action, and in increased sensitivity to other people. In Chelmsford such training is undertaken on a diocesan basis.

It may well be that such work is beyond an individual minister : but planned on an area basis, interdenominationally, such work amongst the local ministering professions would be extremely valuable. This is something which a local council of churches might undertake. And I believe it is important for local churches to take on such work because the ministering professions mostly live at home and, if they go anywhere, go to their local churches. This is increasingly true today of nurses also; and whereas, in the past, Christian organizations working among them may have tried to help through groups and conferences, today the picture is altered by the fact that more hospital staff live out.

In this ministry of healing others, I think it would be fair to say that a great deal of the Church's energy and time is being given to prayer groups for the sick, healing services, and the study of books on 'healing', which ought in fact to be flowing into these new channels of expression. Is it sensible to be praying for an old lady who is bedridden (a clear duty of the Church), but doing little to help the district nurse who cares for her and her family? Who helps them to understand and learn from the spiritual crisis into which senile dementia and facing death have led them? We are better at proclaiming the gospel for the weak than the strong; for the sick than the 'healthy'. We are better at weeping with those who weep than we are at rejoicing with those who rejoice.

Of course we care for our sick and wounded. But St Paul does teach us something when he prayed for the removal of his thorn in the flesh three times only! Although there are times for perseverance in prayer, yet we can make too much of a 'thing' of our intercession groups. And undoubtedly many members of prayer groups are there because of their own spiritual hunger, rather than because of an overflowing of charity for others.

At present there are few opportunities for groups of professional people, who are actually ministering to others, to meet and discuss the problems of their daily work in their own language—seeking Christian answers together. It would be valuable to form on-going seminars to support those who work among people in trouble. It is not necessary for such groups to be exclusively Christian, for real problems have a way of breaking through our differences of approach, and it is good for Christians to contribute their own insights to the discussion.

If you are a Christian nurse and you volunteer for service with the Church in Africa, you may well spend twelve months in a missionary training college, in addition to language study on arrival overseas. If you volunteer for service in a hospital in England (which sounds so much more 'Christian' than merely taking a job) you will get no special training at all. For we only pay lip service to the truth that the Church in Britain is in a missionary situation. Yet conditions of work for a Christian in this country may be more difficult than in many places overseas. To work in a missionary hospital with Christian colleagues has its own difficulties: but the task of evangelism in a hospital in this country is a tough assignment.

It is right to give a nurse going overseas missionary training, in order that she may train nurses in Africa or India. But we also need to give Christian training to the many overseas Christians who come to this country to train as nurses, and return to their own country. Each returning nurse is a key person in her own local community, and is far better placed with regard to language, knowledge of the people and country. Some missionary societies in this country are aware of this need, and are offering overseas nurses in this country the chance to attend a missionary training college alongside English Christians training for overseas.

Once again we must sense new developments in the pattern of the world and penetrate the situation, aware of God at work in it. It is quite clearly a new situation where Britain now has a very large immigrant and student population from all over the world. It is a new situation where today in hospital a dozen or more professions may be personally concerned with the patient, whereas twenty-five years ago the doctor and nurse were almost alone in this ministry.

The Church is already scattered in the world and deeply involved in the life of the world through its laity. We still concentrate on the production of pastors who are ordained ministers, rather than equipping professions who are actually involved and daily being consulted. Of course the priest has his task as pastor : but perhaps we have not yet dared to ask ourselves how far the modern world wants to consult the priest? It may be that for the vast majority of people his ministry can only come through the priesthood of all believers.

SPECIAL ORGANIZATIONS

In the last sixty years there have grown up in this country a profusion of organizations concerned with the healing ministry of the churches : the Guild of Health, the Guild of St Raphael, the Divine Healing Mission, the London Healing Mission, the World-wide Healing Crusade, etc., as well as societies within each church—for example, Methodist, Congregational, Presbyterian and Quaker spiritual healing movements. Their valuable work of healing and teaching is slowly bringing local churches to see this work as a normal part of their task.

The Churches' Council of Healing links up many of these organizations with the medical and nursing professions, in a way which enables it to bring together leading members of the organizations concerned with healing. There will always be a place for specialists, special organizations, and special Homes of Christian Healing in this field of work. But they are not the Church's ministry of healing—only one part of it. An organization like the Samaritans, for example, can undertake special work among suicides where a local church might find difficulty in mobilizing sufficient resources. But how much easier the work of the Samaritans would be if there were more churches able to give real 'family help' to the despairing!

The present pattern of a multiplicity of special organizations tends to confuse our work. As long as they continue, the healing ministry will seem to be something apart from the ordinary life of the church-community, focused upon cure of the sick. The very existence of a Churches' Council of Healing divorces this work from other work in the church which is just as healing. The time will perhaps come when the work of the Churches' Council of Healing will find its place alongside the work for refugees (for example) as *one* of the social concerns of the World Council of Churches.

The foundation of the Institute of Religion and Medicine in 1964 has begun to influence the direction of doctor–clergy co-operation in England. In particular the new Institute has brought into this field a higher standard of intellectual thought, wider possibilities of dialogue, and a more realistic attention to what God is doing in the world today. The participation of other professions associated with medicine, and members from a wider number of faiths are valuable features of the Institute's work.

According to the hopes and fears of nations so we tend to follow certain fashions in concern for different problems. The causes for this run deep. But it may be no coincidence that a world living under the shadow of the Bomb, over-concerns itself with the prolongation of life. Hence healing is fashionable. But sickness is only one manifestation of the human predicament in general, and the Church's work of healing badly needs a transfusion of ideas from those dealing with other symptoms of man's estrangement in the world—hunger, war, *apartheid* and delinquency.

CONCLUSION

'I have come that men may have life, and may have it in all its fullness.'[1]

We rejoice as twentieth-century men and women in the knowledge and skills and way of life which God gives to us each day.

We have only described one aspect of the good life; caring for the sick. There are many people who do not require such help. This book has had no space in which to describe how to live and love and dance with them.

Evil is one, but its symptoms are many. Our conception of healing must be wide enough to include sickness, sin, famine in the Congo, and *apartheid* between races.

The basic causes of ill-health are still largely unknown, but the Church already has an important task in the promotion of health and the prevention of sickness. Little space has been given to this, because by deliberate choice this book is about rehabilitation.

Victory over sickness or handicap does not always lie through healing. In choosing the subject of healing we have presented only one among the several responses to suffering which the Bible describes. Hope, trust and endurance are also ways to fullness of life.

[1] John 10.10.

SELECTED BIBLIOGRAPHY

I. COMPREHENSIVE STUDIES

1. Lambourne, R. A. *Community, Church and Healing* (Darton, Longman & Todd, 1963).
2. Weatherhead, L. *Psychology, Religion and Healing* (Hodder & Stoughton, 1951).
3. Garlick, P. *Man's Search for Health* (Highway Press, 1952).

II. THE KINGDOM OF GOD; HEALING; MIRACLES

4. Fuller, R. H. *Interpreting the Miracles* (SCM Press, 1963).
5. Hoch, D. *Healing and Salvation* (SCM Press, 1958).
6. Richardson, A. *The Miracle Stories of the Gospels* (SCM Press, 1941).
7. Robinson, J. A. T. *On Being the Church in the World* (Chap. 10: 'The Gospel and Health') (SCM Press, 1960).
8. Tillich, P. *Systematic Theology* (vol. 1, pp. 128-130) (Nisbet, 1957).
9. Wilson, J. V. *Go Preach the Kingdom, Heal the Sick* (James Clarke, 1962).
10. Richardson, A. *A Theological Word Book of the Bible*, see under 'Heal' (SCM Press, 1950).

III. HEALING IN THE EARLY CHURCH

11. Frost, E. *Christian Healing* (Mowbray, 1940).
12. McEwen, J. S. *Scottish Journal of Theology* (June 1954).

IV. WORK OF THE LOCAL CHURCH TODAY

(a) *The Congregation*

(See especially: Lambourne, R. A. (1) above; Tübingen Consultation (41) below.)

13. Kenrick, B. *Come Out the Wilderness* (Fontana, 1965 (1962)).
14. Clinebell, H. J. (Junior). *Mental Health through Christian Community* (USA, 1965).
15. Martin, D. V. *The Church as a Healing Community* (Guild of Health, 1958).
16. Warren, M. A. *Partnership* (SCM Press, 1956).
17. Bonhoeffer, D. *The Cost of Discipleship* (SCM Press, 1948).
18. Taylor, J. *The Healing Community* (CMS News-letter, No. 277, 1964).

(b) *Prayer*

19. Wyon, O. *The School of Prayer* (SCM Press, 1957).
20. Head, D. *Stammerer's Tongue* (pp. 59-80, 'Is any afflicted?') (Epworth Press, 1960).
21. Quoist, M. *Prayers of Life* (Gill and Son, Dublin, 1963).
22. Joyce, C. R. B., and Welldon, R. M. C. 'The Objective Efficacy of Prayer—A Double-blind Clinical Trial' (*Journal of Chronic Diseases*, 1965, vol. 18, pp. 367-377).

(c) *Pastoral Work; Counsel; Sacraments*

23. Autton, N. *Pastoral Care of the Mentally Ill* (SPCK, 1963).
24. Kyle, W. H. *Healing through Counselling* (Epworth Press, 1964).
25. Puller, F. W. *Anointing of the Sick in Scripture and Tradition* (Church Historical Society, 1910).

26. Fox, P. *The Church's Ministry of Healing* (Longmans, 1959).
27. Halmos, P. *The Faith of the Counsellors* (Constable, 1965).
28. Clarke, W. K. L. *Liturgy and Worship.* (See Chap. by C. Harris, 'Visitation of the Sick'.) This is a classic (SPCK, 1954).
29. Tournier, P. *The Meaning of Persons* (SCM Press, 1957).
30. Saunders, C. *The Care of the Dying* (*Nursing Times* Reprint, Macmillan, 1959).

V. GROUP DYNAMICS; THERAPEUTIC COMMUNITY; LOVE AND RELATIONSHIPS

(See especially Lambourne, R. A. (1) above; Clinebell, H. J. (Junior) (14) above; Martin, D. V. (15) above.)

31. Rice, K. *Learning for Leadership* (Tavistock Publications, 1965).
32. Martin, D. V. *Adventure in Psychiatry* (Bruno Cassirer, 1962).
33. Bowlby, J. *Child Care and the Growth of Love* (Penguin, 1953).

VI. SUFFERING

34. Tillich, P. *Systematic Theology*, vol. II (see pp. 81-83) (Nisbet, 1957).
35. de Chardin, Teilhard. *Le Milieu Divin* (Collins, 1960).
36. de Beausobre, J. *Creative Suffering* (Dacre, 1940).
37. James, J. *Why Evil?* (Penguin, 1960).

VII. VARIOUS REPORTS

38. *Christianity and Nursing Today* (Epworth Press, 1964).
39. *Clergy–Doctor Co-operation* (Archbishop's Commission) (Church Information Office, 1963).

40. *A Survey of Doctor/Clergy Groups* (Institute of Religion and Medicine, 1964).
41. *The Healing Church.* Report of a Consultation at Tübingen (Division of World Mission and Evangelism, WCC, Geneva, 1965).
42. *The Church's Ministry of Healing* (Archbishop's Commission, Church Information Board, 1958).
43. *Divine Healing and Co-operation between Doctors and Clergy* (BMA, 1956).
44. *Spiritual Healing,* Report of the Church of Scotland Commission (St Andrew Press, 1958).

VIII. THE PROFESSIONS CONCERNED WITH HEALING

(See especially Lambourne, R. A. (1) above; Weatherhead, L. (2) above; Halmos, P. (27) above; *Christianity and Nursing Today* (38) above; *Clergy–Doctor Co-operation* (39) above.

45. Wilson, M. *The Christian Nurse* (Edinburgh House Press, 1960).
46. Wilson, M. 'Priest and Doctor' (*Journal of the C. of E. Hospital Chaplain's Fellowship,* Vol. 3, No. 4, Oct. 1963).
47. Crowlesmith, J. *Religion and Medicine* Various essays (Epworth Press, 1962).
48. Revans, R. W. *Standards for Morale: Cause and Effect in Hospitals* (OUP, 1964).
49. Menzies, I. E. P. 'A Case Study in the Functioning of Human Systems as a Defence against Anxiety' (*Human Relations,* 1960, 13, No. 2, pp. 95-121).
50. Balint, M. *The Doctor, the Patient, and the Illness* (Pitman, 1957).

IX. ETHICAL DECISIONS

51. Jenkins, D. T. *The Doctor's Profession* (SCM Press, 1949).
52. Davidson, M. *Medical Ethics* (see Chap. 10, 'What to tell the Gravely Ill Patient'; Chap. 11, 'The Management of the Hopeless Case') (Lloyd-Luke, 1957).
53. Fletcher, J. *Morals and Medicine* (Gollancz, 1955).
54. St John Stevas, N. *Life, Death, and the Law* (Eyre and Spottiswoode, 1961).

A series of Reports on Ethical Questions (Church Information Office). The three most recent publications are:

55. *Decisions about Life and Death*
56. *Abortion—an ethical discussion*
57. *Fatherless by Law*

INDEX